I0129281

Charlotte Mary Yonge, Charlotte Mary Yonge

Stray Pearls

Charlotte Mary Yonge, Charlotte Mary Yonge

Stray Pearls

ISBN/EAN: 9783744670395

Printed in Europe, USA, Canada, Australia, Japan

Cover: Foto ©Thomas Meinert / pixelio.de

More available books at **www.hansebooks.com**

MEMOIRS OF

MARGARET DE RIBAUMONT

VISCOUNTESS OF BELLAISE

BY

CHARLOTTE M. YONGE

AUTHOR OF 'HEIR OF REDCLYFFE,' 'UNKNOWN TO HISTORY,' ETC.

VOL. I.

London

MACMILLAN AND CO.

1883

PREFACE.

No one can be more aware than the author that the construction of this tale is defective. The state of French society, and the strange scenes of the Fronde, beguiled me into a tale which has become rather a family record than a novel.

Formerly the Muse of the historical romance was an independent and arbitrary personage, who could compress time, resuscitate the dead, give mighty deeds to imaginary heroes, exchange substitutes for popular martyrs on the scaffold, and make the most stubborn facts subservient to her purpose. Indeed, her most favoured son boldly asserted her right to bend time and place to her purpose, and to make the interest and effectiveness of her work the paramount object. But critics have lashed her out of these erratic ways, and she is now become the meek handmaid of Clio, creeping obediently in the track of the

a

greater Muse, and never venturing on more than colouring and working up the grand outlines that her mistress
has left undefined. Thus, in the present tale, though it
would have been far more convenient not to have spread
the story over such a length of time, and to have made
the catastrophe depend upon the heroes and heroines,
instead of keeping them mere ineffective spectators, or
only engaged in imaginary adventures for which a precedent can be found, it has been necessary to stretch out
their narrative, so as to be at least consistent with the
real history, at the entire sacrifice of the plot. And it
may be feared that thus the story may partake of the
confusion that really reigned over the tangled thread of
events. There is no portion of history better illustrated
by memoirs of the actors therein than is the Fronde; but,
perhaps, for that very reason none so confusing.

Perhaps it may be an assistance to the reader to lay
out the bare historical outline like a map, showing to
what incidents the memoirs of the Sisters of Ribaumont
have to conform themselves.

When Henry IV. succeeded in obtaining the throne
of France, he found the feudal nobility depressed by the
long civil war, and his exchequer exhausted. He and

his minister Sully returned to the policy of Louis XI., by which the nobles were to be kept down and prevented from threatening the royal power. This was seldom done by violence, but by giving them employment in the Army and Court, attaching them to the person of the King, and giving them offices with pensions attached to them.

The whole cost of these pensions and all the other expenses of Government fell on the townspeople and peasantry, since the clergy and the nobles to all generations were exempt from taxation. The trade and all the resources of the country were taking such a spring of recovery since the country had been at peace, and the persecution of the Huguenots had ceased, that at first the taxation provoked few murmurs. The resources of the Crown were further augmented by permitting almost all magistrates and persons who held public offices to secure the succession to their sons on the payment of a tariff called *la Paulette* from the magistrate who invented it.

In the next reign, however, an effort was made to secure greater equality of burthens. On the meeting of the States-General—the only popular assembly possessed by France—Louis XIII., however, after hearing the com-

plaints, and promising to consider them, shut the doors
against the deputies, made no further answer, and dis-
missed them to their houses without the slightest redress.
The Assembly was never to meet again till the day of
reckoning for all, a hundred and seventy years later.

Under the mighty hand of Cardinal Richelieu the
nobles were still more effectually crushed, and the great
course of foreign war begun, which lasted, with short
intervals, for a century.   The great man died, and so did
his feeble master; and his policy, both at home and
abroad, was inherited by his pupil Giulio Mazarini, while
the regency for the child, Louis XIV., devolved on his
mother, Anne of Austria—a pious and well-meaning,
but proud and ignorant, Spanish Princess—who pinned
her faith upon Mazarin with helpless and exclusive
devotion, believing him the only pilot who could steer
her vessel through troublous waters.

But what France had ill brooked from the high-
handed son of her ancient nobility was intolerable from a
low-born Italian, of graceful but insinuating manners.
Moreover, the war increased the burthens of the country,
and, in the minority of the King, a stand was made at last.

The last semblance of popular institutions existed in

the Parliaments of the Provinces, especially that of Paris. The nucleus of this was the old feudal Council of the Counts of Paris, consisting of the temporal and spiritual peers of the original county, who had the right to advise with their chief, and to try the causes concerning themselves. The immediate vassals of the King had a right to sit there, and were called *Pairs de France*, in distinction from the other nobles who only had seats in the Parliament in whose province their lands might lie. To these St. Louis, in his anxiety to repress lawlessness, had added a certain number of trained lawyers and magistrates; and these were the working members' of these Parliaments, which were in general merely courts of justice for civil and criminal causes. The nobles only attended on occasions of unusual interest. Moreover, a law or edict of the King became valid on being registered by a Parliament. It was a moot question whether the Parliament had the power to baffle the King by refusing to register an edict, and Henry IV. had avoided a refusal from the Parliament of Paris, by getting his edict of toleration for the Huguenots registered at Nantes.

The peculiarly oppressive house-tax, with four more imposts proposed in 1648, gave the Parliament of Paris

the opportunity of trying to make an effectual resistance
by refusing the registration. They were backed by the
municipal government of the city at the Hôtel de Ville,
and encouraged by the Coadjutor of the infirm old Archbishop of Paris, namely, his nephew, Paul de Gondi,
titular Bishop of Corinth *in partibus infidelium*, a younger
son of the Duke of Retz, an exceedingly clever young
man, descended from an Italian family introduced by
Catherine de Medici. There seemed to be a hope that
the nobility, angered at their own systematic depression,
and by Mazarin's ascendency, might make common cause
with the Parliament and establish some effectual check
to the advances of the Crown. This was the origin of
the party called the Fronde, because the speakers launched
their speeches at one another as boys fling stones from a
sling (*fronde*) in the streets.

The Queen-Regent was enraged through all her des-
potic Spanish haughtiness at such resistance. She tried
to step in by the arrest of the foremost members of the
Opposition, but failed, and only provoked violent tumults.
The young Prince of Condé, coming home from Germany
flushed with victory, hated Mazarin extremely, but his
pride as a Prince of the Blood, and his private animosities,

impelled him to take up the cause of the Queen. She conveyed her son secretly from Paris, and the city was in a state of siege for several months. However, the execution of Charles I. in England alarmed the Queen on the one hand, and the Parliament on the other, as to the con- sequences of a rebellion, provisions began to run short, and a vague hollow peace was made in the March of 1649.

Condé now became intolerably overbearing, insulted every one, and so much offended the Queen and Mazarin that they caused him, his brother, and the Duke of Bouillon, to be arrested and imprisoned at Vincennes. His wife, though a cruelly-neglected woman whom he had never loved, did her utmost to deliver him, repaired to Bordeaux, and gained over the Parliament there, so that she held out four months against the Queen. Turenne, brother to Bouillon, and as great a general as Condé, obtained the aid of the Spaniards, and the Coadjutor prevailed on the King's uncle, Gaston, Duke of Orléans, to represent that the Queen must give way, release the Princes, part with Mazarin, and even promise to convoke the States-General. Anne still, however, corresponded with the Cardinal, and was directed by him in everything. Distrust and dissension soon broke out, Condé and the Coadjutor quarrelled violently, and the royal promises made to both Princes and Parliament were eluded by the King, at fourteen, being declared to have attained his majority, and thus that all engagements made in his name became void.

Condé went off to Guienne and raised an army; Mazarin returned to the Queen; Paris shut its gates and declared Mazarin an outlaw. The Coadjutor (now become Cardinal de Retz) vainly tried to stir up the Duke of Orléans to take a manly part and mediate between the parties; but being much afraid of his own appanage, the city of Orléans, being occupied by either army, Gaston sent his daughter to take the charge of it, as she effectually did—but she was far from neutrality, being deluded by a hope that Condé would divorce his poor faithful wife to marry her. Turenne, on his brother's release, had made his peace with the Court, and commanded the royal army. War and havoc raged outside Paris; within the partisans of the Princes stirred the populace to endeavour to intimidate the Parliament and municipality into taking their part. Their chief leader throughout was the Duke of Beaufort, a younger son of the Duke of

Vendôme, the child of Gabrielle d'Estrées. He inherited his grandmother's beauty and his grandfather's charm of manner; he was the darling of the populace of Paris, and led them, in an aimless sort of way, wherever there was mischief to be done; and the violence and tumult of this latter Fronde were far worse than those of the first.

A terrible battle in the Faubourg St. Antoine broke Condé's force, and the remnant was only saved by Mademoiselle's insisting on their being allowed to pass through Paris. After one ungrateful attempt to terrify the magistrates into espousing his cause and standing a siege on his behalf, Condé quitted Paris, and soon after fell ill of a violent fever.

His party melted away. Mazarin saw that tranquillity might be restored if he quitted France for a time. The King proclaimed an amnesty, but with considerable exceptions and no relaxation of his power; and these terms the Parliament, weary of anarchy, and finding the nobles had cared merely for their personal hatreds, not for the public good, were forced to accept.

Condé, on his recovery, left France, and for a time fought against his country in the ranks of the Spaniards.

Beaufort died bravely fighting against the Turks at Cyprus. Cardinal de Retz was imprisoned, and Mademoiselle had to retire from Court, while other less distinguished persons had to undergo the punishment for their resistance, though, to the credit of the Court party be it spoken, there were no executions, only imprisonments; and in after years the Fronde was treated as a brief frenzy, and forgotten.

Perhaps it may be well to explain that Mademoiselle was Anne Geneviève de Bourbon, daughter of Gaston, Duke of Orléans, by his first wife, the heiress of the old Bourbon branch of Montpensier. She was the greatest heiress in France, and an exceedingly vain and eccentric person, aged twenty-three at the beginning of the Fronde.

It only remains to say that I have no definite authority for introducing such a character as that of Clément Darpent, but it is well known that there was a strong under-current of upright, honest, and highly-cultivated men among the *bourgeoisie* and magistrates, and that it seemed to me quite possible that in the first Fronde, when the Parliament were endeavouring to make a stand for a just right, and hoping to obtain further freedom, a young and educated man might entertain further hopes and schemes, and, acting on higher and purer principles than those around him, be universally misunderstood and suspected.

C. M. YONGE.

CONTENTS OF VOL. 1.

CHAPTER I.

CHAPTER II.

CHAPTER III.

CHAPTER IV.

CHAPTER V.

CHAPTER VI.

CHAPTER VII.

CHAPTER VIII.

CHAPTER IX.

CHAPTER X.

CHAPTER XI.

CHAPTER XII.

CHAPTER XIII.

CHAPTER XIV.

CHAPTER XV.

CHAPTER XVI.

CHAPTER XVII.

CHAPTER XVIII.

STRAY PEARLS.

THE MEMOIRS OF MARGARET DE RIBAUMONT, VISCOUNTESS OF BELLAISE.

CHAPTER I.

WHITEHALL BEFORE THE COBWEBS.

I HAVE long promised you, my dear grandchildren, to arrange my recollections of the eventful years that even your father can hardly remember. I shall be glad thus to draw closer the bonds between ourselves and the English kindred, whom I love so heartily, though I may never hope to see them again in this world, far less the dear old home where I grew up.

For, as perhaps you have forgotten, I am an Englishwoman by birth, having first seen the light at Walwyn House, in Dorsetshire. One brother had preceded me—my dear Eustace—and another brother, Berenger, and my little sister, Annora, followed me.

Our family had property both in England and in Picardy, and it was while attending to some business

connected with the French estate that my father had
fallen in love with a beautiful young widow, Madame la
Baronne de Solivet (*née* Cheverny), and had brought her
home, in spite of the opposition of her relations.   I cannot tell whether she were warmly welcomed at Walwyn
Court by any one but the dear beautiful grandmother, a
Frenchwoman herself, who was delighted again to hear
her mother tongue, although she had suffered much among
the Huguenots in her youth, when her husband was left
for dead on the S. Barthélémi.

He, my grandfather, had long been dead, but I perfectly remember her.   She used to give me a sugar-cake
when I said " *Bon soir, bonne maman,*" with the right
accent, and no one made sugar-cakes like hers.   She
always wore at her girdle a string of little yellow shells,
which she desired to have buried with her.   We children
were never weary of hearing how they had been the only
traces of her or of her daughter that her husband could
find, when he came to the ruined city.

I could fill this book with her stories, but I must not
linger over them; and indeed I heard no more after I
was eight years old.   Until that time my brother and I
were left under her charge in the country, while my
father and mother were at court.   My mother was one
of the Ladies of the Bedchamber to Queen Henrietta
Maria, who had been enchanted to find in her a country-
woman, and of the same faith.   I was likewise bred up

in their Church, my mother having obtained the consent
of my father, during a dangerous illness that followed my
birth, but the other children were all brought up as
Protestants.   Indeed, no difference was made between
Eustace and me when we were at Walwyn.   Our grandmother taught us both alike to make the sign of the cross,
and likewise to say our prayers and the catechism ; and
oh ! we loved her very much.

Eustace once gave two black eyes to our rude cousin,
Harry Merricourt, for laughing when he said no one was
as beautiful as the grandmother, and though I am an old
woman myself, I think he was right.   She was like a
little fairy, upright and trim, with dark flashing eyes,
that never forgot how to laugh, and snowy curls on her
brow.

I believe that the dear old lady made herself ill by
nursing us two children day and night when we had the
smallpox.   She had a stroke, and died before my father
could be fetched from London ; but I knew nothing of
all that ; I only grieved, and wondered that she did not
come to me, till at last the maid who was nursing me told
me flatly that the old lady was dead.   I think that afterwards we were sent down to a farmer's house by the
sea, to be bathed and made rid of the infection ; and
that the pleasure of being set free from our sick cham-
bers and of playing on the shore drove from our minds
for the time our grief for the good grandam, though

indeed I dream of her often still, and of the old rooms and gardens at Walwyn, though I have never seen them since.

When we were quite well and tolerably free from pock-marks, my father took us to London with him, and there Eustace was sent to school at Westminster; while I, with little Berry, had a tutor to teach us Latin and French, and my mother's waiting-maid instructed me in sewing and embroidery. As I grew older I had masters in dancing and the spinnet, and my mother herself was most careful of my deportment. Likewise she taught me such practices of our religion as I had not learnt from my grandmother, and then it was I found that I was to be brought up differently from Eustace and the others. I cried at first, and declared I would do like Eustace and my father, but no one would listen to me, not even my father. I did not think much about it; I was too childish and thoughtless to be really devout; and when my mother took me in secret to the queen's little chapel, full of charming objects of devotion, while the others had to sit still during sermons two hours long, I began to think that I was the best off.

Since that time I have thought much more, and talked the subject over both with my dear eldest brother and with good priests, both English and French, and I have come to the conclusion, as you know, my children, that the English doctrine is no heresy, and that the

Church is a true Church and Catholic, though, as my
home and my duties lie here, I remain where I was
brought up by my mother, in the communion of my
husband and children.   I know that this would seem
almost heresy to our good Père Chavand, but I wish to
leave my sentiments on record for you, my children.

But how I have anticipated my history! I must
return, to tell you that when I was just sixteen I was
told that I was to go to my first ball at Whitehall.   My
hair was curled over my forehead, and I was dressed in
white satin, with the famous pearls of Ribaumont round
my neck, though of course they were not to be mine
eventually.

I knew the palace well, having often had the honour
of playing with the Lady Mary, who was some years
younger than I, so that I was much less alarmed than
many young gentlewomen there making their first appearance.   But, as my dear brother Eustace led me into the
outer hall, close behind my father and mother, I heard a
strange whistle, and, looking up, I saw over the balus-
trade of the gallery a droll monkey face looking out of a
mass of black curls, and making significant grimaces at
me.

I knew well enough that it was no other than the
Prince of Wales.   He was terribly ugly and fond of
teasing, but in a good-natured way, always leaving off
when he saw he was giving real pain, and I liked him

much better than his brother, the Duke of York, who was proud and sullen. Yet one could always trust the Duke, and that could not be said for the Prince.

By the time we had slowly advanced up the grand staircase into the banqueting-hall, and had made our reverences to the king and queen—ah, how stately and beautiful they looked together!—the Prince had stepped in some other way, and stood beside me.

"Well, Meg," he said, in an undertone—"I beg pardon, Mrs. Margaret—decked out in all her splendour, a virgin for the sacrifice!"

"What sacrifice, sir?" I asked, startled.

"Eh!" he said. "You do not know that *le futur* is arrived!"

"She knows nothing, your Highness," said Eustace.

"What, oh, what is there to know?" I implored the Prince and my brother in turn to inform me, for I saw that there was some earnest in the Prince's jests, and I knew that the queen and my mother were looking out for a good match for me in France.

"Let me show him to you," presently whispered the Prince, who had been called off by his father to receive the civilities of an ambassador. Then he pointed out a little wizened dried-up old man, who was hobbling up to kiss Her Majesty's hand, and whose courtly smile seemed to me to sit most unnaturally on his wrinkled countenance. I nearly screamed. I was forced to bite my lips to keep back my tears, and I wished myself child enough to be able to scream and run away, when my mother presently beckoned me forward. I hardly had strength to curtsey when I was actually presented to the old man. Nothing but terror prevented my sinking on the floor, and I heard as through falling waters something about M. le Marquis de Nidemerle and Mrs. Margaret Ribmont, for so we were called in England.

By and by I found that I was dancing, I scarcely knew how or with whom, and I durst not look up the whole time, nor did my partner address a single word to me, though I knew he was near me ; I was only too thankful that he did not try to address me.

To my joy, when we had made our final reverences, he never came near me again all the evening. I found myself among some young maidens who were friends of mine, and in our eager talk together I began to forget what had passed, or to hope it was only some teasing pastime of the Prince and Eustace.

When we were seated in the coach on the way to our house my father began to laugh and marvel which had been the most shy, the gallant or the lady, telling my mother she need never reproach the English with bash-fulness again after this French specimen.

" How will he and little Meg ever survive to-morrow's meeting!" he said.

Then I saw it was too true, and cried out in despair

to beg them to let me stay at home, and not send me from them ; but my mother bade me not be a silly wench. I had always known that I was to be married in France, and the queen and my half-brother, M. de Solivet, had found an excellent *parti* for me. I was not to embarrass matters by any folly, but I must do her credit, and not make her regret that she had not sent me to a convent to be educated.

Then I clung to my father. I could hold him tight in the dark, and the flambeaux only cast in a fitful flickering light. " Oh, sir," said I, "you cannot wish to part with your little Meg !"

" You are your mother's child, Meg," he said sadly. " I gave you up to her to dispose of at her will."

" And you will thank me one of these days for your secure home," said my mother. " If these rogues continue disaffected, who knows what they may leave us in England !"

" At least we should be together," I cried, and I remember how I fondled my father's hand in the dark, and how he returned it. We should never have thought of such a thing in the light; he would have been ashamed to allow such an impertinence, and I to attempt it.

Perhaps it emboldened me to say timidly : " If he were not so old——"

But my mother declared that she could not believe

her ears that a child of hers should venture on making such objections—so unmaidenly, so undutiful to a *parti* selected by the queen and approved by her parents.

As the coach stopped at our own door I perceived that certain strange noises that I had heard proceeded from Eustace laughing and chuckling to himself all the way. I must say I thought it very unkind and cruel when we had always loved each other so well. I would hardly bid him good-night, but ran up to the room I shared with nurse and Annora, and wept bitterly through half the night, little comforted by nurse's assurance that old men were wont to let their wives have their way far more easily than young ones did.

CHAPTER II.

A LITTLE MUTUAL AVERSION.

I HAD cried half the night, and when in the morning
little Nan wanted to hear about my ball, I only answered
that I hated the thought of it. I was going to be
married to a hideous old man, and be carried to France,
and should never see any of them again. I made Nan
cry too, and we both came down to breakfast with such
mournful faces that my mother chid me sharply for
making myself such a fright.

Then she took me away to the still-room, and set
me for an hour to make orange cakes, while she gave
orders for the great dinner that we were to give that
day, I knew only too well for whose sake; and if I had
only known which orange cake was for my betrothed,
would not it have been a bitter one! By and by my
mother carried me off to be dressed. She never trusted
the tiring-woman to put the finishing touches with those
clumsy English fingers; and, besides, she bathed my
swollen eyelids with essences, and made me rub my pale

cheeks with a scarlet ribbon, speaking to me so sharply that I should not have dared to shed another tear.

When I was ready, all in white, and she, most stately in blue velvet and gold, I followed her down the stairs to the grand parlour, where stood my father, with my brothers and one or two persons in black, who I found were a notary and his clerk, and there was a table before them with papers, parchment, a standish, and pens. I believe if it had been a block, and I had had to lay my head on it, like poor Lady Jane Grey, I could not have been much more frightened.

There was a sound of wheels, and presently the gentleman usher came forward, announcing the Most Noble the Marquis de Nidemerle, and the Lord Viscount of Bellaise. My father and brothers went half-way down the stairs to meet them, my mother advanced across the room, holding me in one hand and Annora in the other. We all curtsied low, and as the gentlemen advanced, bowing low, and almost sweeping the ground with the plumes in their hats, we each had to offer them a cheek to salute after the English fashion. The old marquis was talking French so fast that I could not understand him in the least, but somehow a mist suddenly seemed to clear away from before me, and I found that I was standing before that alarming table, not with him, but with something much younger—not much older, indeed, than Eustace.

I began to hear what the notary was reading out, and behold it was—" Contract of marriage on the part of Philippe Marie François de Bellaise, Marquis de Nidemerle, and Eustace de Ribaumont, Baron Walwyn of Walwyn, in Dorset, and Baron de Ribaumont in Picardy, on behoof of Gaspard Henri Philippe, Viscount de Bellaise, nephew of the Marquis de Nidemerle, and Margaret Henrietta Maria de Ribaumont, daughter of the Baron de Ribaumont."

Then I knew that I had been taken in by the Prince's wicked trick, and that my husband was to be the young viscount, not the old uncle! I do not think that this was much comfort to me at the moment, for, all the same, I was going into a strange country, away from every one I had ever known.

But I did take courage to look up under my eyelashes at the form I was to see with very different eyes. M. de Bellaise was only nineteen, but although not so tall as my father or brother, he had already that grand military bearing which is only acquired in the French service, and no wonder, for he had been three years in the Regiment de Condé, and had already seen two battles and three sieges in Savoy, and now had only leave of absence for the winter before rejoining his regiment in the Low Countries.

Yet he looked as bashful as a maiden. It was true that, as my father said, his bashfulness was as great as an Englishman's. Indeed, he had been bred up at his great uncle's château in Anjou, under a strict abbé who had gone with him to the war, and from whom he was only now to be set free upon his marriage. He had scarcely ever spoken to any lady but his old aunt—his parents had long been dead—and he had only two or three times seen his little sister through the grating of her convent. So, as he afterwards confessed, nothing but his military drill and training bore him through the affair. He stood upright as a dart, bowed at the right place, and in due time signed his name to the contract, and I had to do the same. Then there ensued a great state dinner, where he and I sat together, but neither of us spoke to the other; and when, as I was trying to see the viscount under my eyelashes, I caught his eyes trying to do the same by me, I remember my cheeks flaming all over, and I think his must have done the same, for my father burst suddenly out into a laugh without apparent cause, though he tried to check himself when he saw my mother's vexation.

When all was over, she highly lauded the young gentleman, declaring that he was an example of the decorum with which such matters were conducted in France; and when my father observed that he should prefer a little more fire and animation, she said: "Truly, my lord, one would think you were of mere English extraction, that you should prefer the rude habits of a farmer or milkmaid to the reserve of a true noble and lady of quality."

"Well, dame, I promised that you should have it your own way with the poor lass," said my father; "and I see no harm in the lad, but I own I should like to know more of him, and Meg would not object either. It was not the way I took thee, Margaret."

"I shall never make you understand that a widow is altogether a different thing," said my mother.

I suppose they never recollected that I could hear every word they said, but I was full in view of them, and of course I was listening most anxiously for all I could gather about my new life. If I remember right, it was an envoy-extraordinary with whom the marquis and his nephew had come, and their stay was therefore very short, so that we were married after a very few days in the Queen's Chapel, by her own almoner.

I do not remember much about the wedding, as indeed it was done very quietly, being intended to be kept altogether a secret; but in some way, probably through the servants, it became known to the mob in London, and as we drove home from Whitehall in the great coach with my father and mother, a huge crowd had assembled, hissing and yelling and crying out upon Lord Walwyn for giving his daughter to a French Papist.

The wretches! they even proceeded to throw stones. My young bridegroom saw one of these which would have

struck me had he not thrown himself forward, holding up
his hat as a shield. The stone struck him in the eye,
and he dropped forward upon my mother's knee senseless.

The crowd were shocked then, and fell back, but
what good did that do to him? He was carried to his
chamber, and a surgeon was sent for, who said that there
was no great injury done, for the eye itself had not been
touched, but that he must be kept perfectly quiet until
the last minute, if he was to be able to travel without danger,
when the suite were to set off in two days' time. They
would not let me go near him. Perhaps I was relieved, for
I should not have known what to do; yet I feared that he
would think me unkind and ungrateful, and I would have
begged my mother and Eustace to thank him and make
my excuses, but I was too shy, and I felt it very hard to
be blamed for indifference and rudeness.

Indeed, we four young ones kept as much together as
we could do in the house and gardens, and played all our
dear old games of shuttlecock, and pig go to market, and
proverbs, and all that you, my children, call very English
sports, because we knew only too well that we should
never play at them together again. The more I was
blamed for being childish, the more I was set upon them,
till at last my mother said that she was afraid to let me
go, I was so childish and unfeeling; and my father replied
that she should have thought of that before. He and I
were both more English at heart than French, and I am

sure now that he perceived better than I did myself that
my clinging to my brothers and sister, and even my noisy
merriment, were not the effect of want of feeling.

As to my bridegroom, I have since known that he
was dreadfully afraid of us, more especially of me, and
was thankful that the injury kept him a prisoner. Nay,
he might have come downstairs, if he had been willing,
on the last evening, but he shrank from another pre-
sentation to me before the eyes of all the world, and
chose instead to act the invalid, with no companion save
Eustace, with whom he had made friends.

I will not tell you about the partings, and the
promises and assurances that we should meet again. My
father had always promised that my mother should see
France once more, and he now declared that they would
all visit me. Alas! we little thought what would be
the accomplishment of that promise.

My father and Eustace rode with us from London to
Dover, and all that time I kept close to them. M. de
Bellaise was well enough to ride too. His uncle, the
marquis, went in a great old coach with the ladies, wives
of some of his suite, and I should have been there too,
but that I begged so hard to ride with my father that
he yielded, after asking M. le Vicomte whether he had
any objection. M. le Vicomte opened great eyes, smiled,
blushed and bowed, stammering something. I do not think
that he had quite realised previously that I was his wife,

and belonged to him. My father made him ride with us, and talked to him; and out in the open air, riding with the wind in our cheeks, and his plume streaming in the breeze, he grew much less shy, and began to talk about the wolf-hunts and boar-hunts in the Bocage, and of all the places that my father and I both knew as well as if we had seen them, from the grandam's stories.

I listened, but we neither of us sought the other; indeed, I believe it seemed hard to me that when there was so little time with my father and Eustace, they should waste it on these hunting stories. Only too soon we were at Dover, and the last, last farewell and blessing were given. I looked my last, though I knew it not, at that dear face of my father!

CHAPTER III.

CELADON AND CHLOE.

MY tears were soon checked by dreadful sea-sickness.
We were no sooner out of Dover than the cruel wind
turned round upon us, and we had to go beating about
with all our sails reefed for a whole day and night before
it was safe to put into Calais.

All that time I was in untold misery, and poor nurse
Tryphena was worse than I was, and only now and then
was heard groaning out that she was a dead woman, and
begging me to tell some one to throw her overboard.

But it was that voyage which gave me my husband.
He was not exactly at his ease, but he kept his feet
better than any of the other gentlemen, and he set himself to supply the place of valet to his uncle, and of maid
to me, going to and fro between our cabins as best he
could, for he fell and rolled whenever he tried to move;
and he never stayed five minutes by my side before a
sharp shriek or howl, or a message through the steward,
summoned him back to M. le Marquis, who had utterly

forgotten all his politeness and formality towards the
ladies.

However, our sufferings were over at last. My husband, who was by this time bruised from head to foot by
his falls, though he made no complaints, came to say we
should in a few moments be in port. He helped me to
dress, for Tryphena thought she was dead, and would not
move; and he dragged me on deck, where the air revived
me, and where one by one the whole party appeared,
spectacles of misery.

M. le Marquis did not recover himself till he was
on shore, and caused himself to be assisted to the quay
between his nephew and the valet, leaving me to myself;
but the dear viscount returned for me, and after he had
set me ashore, as he saw I was anxious about Tryphena,
he went back and fetched her, as carefully as if she had
been a lady, in spite of the grumblings of his uncle and
of her own refractoriness, for she was horribly frightened,
and could not understand a word he said to her.

Nevertheless, as soon as we had all of us come to
ourselves, it turned out that he had gained her heart.
Indeed, otherwise I should have had to send her home,
for she pined sadly for some time, and nothing but her
love for me and her enthusiastic loyalty to him kept her
up during the first months.

As to my husband and me, that voyage had made us
as fond of one another's company on one side of the

Channel as we had been afraid of it before on the other, but there was no more riding together for us. I had to travel in the great coach with M. le Marquis, the three ladies, and all our women, where I was so dull and weary that I should have felt ready to die, but for watching for my husband's plume, or now and then getting a glance and a nod from him as he rode among the other gentlemen, braving all their laughter at his devotion; for, bashful as he was, he knew how to hold his own.

I knew that the ladies looked on me as an ugly little rustic foreigner, full of English *mauvaise honte.* If they tried to be kind to me, it was as a mere child ; and they went on with their chatter, which I could hardly follow, for it was about things and people of which I knew nothing, so that I could not understand their laughter. Or when they rejoiced in their return from what they called their exile, and found fault with all they had left in England, my cheeks burned with indignation.

My happy hours were when we halted for refreshments. My husband handed me to my place at table and sat beside me; or he would walk with me about the villages where we rested. The ladies were shocked, and my husband was censured for letting me *"faire l'Anglaise;"* but we were young and full of spirits, and the being thus thrown on each other had put an end to his timidity towards me. He did indeed blush up to his curls, and hold himself as upright as a ramrod, when satire was

directed to us as Celadon and Chloe ; but he never took
any other notice of it, nor altered his behaviour in consequence.   Indeed, we felt like children escaping from
school when we crept down the stairs in early morning,
and hand-in-hand repaired to the church in time for the
very earliest mass among the peasants, who left their
scythes at the door, and the women with their *hottes*, or
their swaddled babies at their backs.   We would get a
cup of milk and piece of barley-bread at some cottage,
and wander among the orchards, fields, or vineyards
before Mesdames had begun their toilets ; and when we
appeared at the *déjeûner*, the gentlemen would compliment me on my *rouge au naturel*, and the ladies would
ironically envy my English appetite.

Sometimes we rested in large hostels in cities, and
then our walk began with some old cathedral, which
could not but be admired, Gothic though it were, and
continued in the market-place, where the piles of fruit,
vegetables, and flowers were a continual wonder and
delight to me.   My husband would buy bouquets of
pinks and roses for me ; but in the coach the ladies
always said they incommoded them by their scent,
and obliged me to throw them away.   The first day
I could not help shedding a few tears, for I feared
he would think I did not value them ; and then I
perceived that they thought the little Englishwoman a
child crying for her flowers.   I longed to ask them

whether they had ever loved their husbands; but I knew how my mother would have looked at me, and forbore.

Once or twice we were received in state at some château, where our mails had to be opened that we might sup in full toilet; but this was seldom, for most of the equals of M. le Marquis lived at Paris. Sometimes our halt was at an abbey, where we ladies were quartered in a guest-chamber without; and twice we slept at large old convents, where nobody had lived since the Huguenot times, except a lay brother put in by M. l'Abbé to look after the estate and make the house a kind of inn for travellers. There were fine walled gardens run into wild confusion, and little neglected and dismantled shrines, and crosses here and there, with long wreaths of rose and honeysuckle trailing over them, and birds' nests in curious places. My Viscount laughed with a new pleasure when I showed him the wren's bright eye peeping out from her nest, and he could not think how I knew the egg of a hedge-sparrow from that of a red-breast. Even he had never been allowed to be out of sight of his tutor, and he knew none of these pleasures so freely enjoyed by my brothers; while as to his sister Cécile, she had been carried from her nurse to a convent, and had thence been taken at fourteen to be wedded to the grandson and heir of the Count d'Aubépine, who kept the young couple under their own eye at their castle in the Bocage.

My husband had absolutely only seen her twice, and then through the grating, and the marriage had taken place while he was in Savoy last autumn. He knew his brother-in-law a little better, having been his neighbour at Nid de Merle; but he shrugged his shoulders as he spoke of "*le chevalier*," and said he was very young, adored by his grandparents, and rather headstrong.

As to growing up together in the unity that had always existed between Eustace and me, he had never heard or dreamt of such a thing; and he confessed that it had been an absolute surprise to him to find that my dear brother was grieved at parting with me. He said he had lain and heard our shouts in the passages with wonder as we played those old games of ours.

"As though you were in a den of roaring wild beasts," I said; for I ventured on anything with him by that time, and when he tried to say they were wild beasts with sweet voices, I teased him about his feelings at having to carry off one of these same savage beasts with him; and then he told me how surprised he had been when, on the last evening he spent in his chamber in our house, Eustace had come and implored him to be good to me, telling him —ah, I can see my dear brother's boyish way!—all my best qualities, ranging from my always speaking truth to my being able to teach the little dog to play tricks, and warning him of what vexed or pained me, even exacting a promise that he would take care of me when I was

away from them all. I believe that promise was foremost in my husband's mind when he waited on me at sea.
Nay, he said when he remembered the tears in my brother's
eyes, and saw how mine arose at the thought, his heart
smote him when he remembered that his sister's marriage
had scarcely cost him a thought or care, and that she was
an utter stranger to him; and then we agreed that if
ever we had children, we would bring them up to know
and love one another, and have precious recollections in
common. Ah! *l'homme propose, mais Dieu dispose.*

It was only on that day that it broke upon me that
we were to be separated immediately after our arrival in
Paris. M. de Bellaise was to go to his regiment, which
was in garrison at Nancy, and I was to be left under the
charge of old Madame la Marquise de Nidemerle at Paris.
I heard of it first from the Marquis himself in the coach,
as he thanked one of the ladies who invited me—with
him—to her *salon* in Paris, where there was to be a great
entertainment in the summer. When I replied that M.
de Bellaise would have rejoined his regiment, they began
explaining that I should go into society under Madame
de Nidemerle, who would exert herself for my sake.

I said no more. I knew it was of no use there; but
when next I could speak with my husband—it was
under an arbour of vines in the garden of the inn where
we dined—I asked him whether it was true. He opened
large eyes, and said he knew I could not wish to with-

draw him from his duty to his king and country, even if he could do so with honour.

"Ah! no," I said; "I never thought of that." But surely the place of a wife was with her husband, and I had expected to go with him to his garrison at Nancy, and there wait when he took the field. He threw himself at my feet, and pressed my hands with transport at what he called this unheard-of proof of affection; and then I vexed him by laughing, for I could not help thinking what my brothers would have said, could they have seen us thus.

Still he declared that, in spite of his wishes, it was hardly possible. His great-uncle and aunt would never consent. I said they had no right to interfere between husband and wife, and he replied that they had brought him up, and taken the place of parents to him; to which I rejoined that I was far nearer to him. He said I was a mutinous Englishwoman; and I rejoined that he should never find me mutinous to him.

Nay, I made up my mind that if he would not insist on taking me, I would find means to escape and join him. What! Was I to be carried about in the coach of Madame de Nidemerle to all the hateful *salons* of Paris, while my husband, the only person in France whom I could endure, might be meeting wounds and death in the Low Countries while I might be dancing!

So again I declined when the ladies in the coach

invited me to their houses in Paris. Should I go to a
convent? they asked; and one began to recommend the
Carmelites, another the Visitation, another Port Royal,
till I was almost distracted; and M. le Marquis began to
say it was a pious and commendable wish, but that
devotion had its proper times and seasons, and that
judgment must be exercised as to the duration of a
retreat, etc.

" No, Monsieur," said I, "I am not going into a convent. A wife's duty is with her husband; I am going
into garrison at Nancy."

Oh, how they cried out! There was such a noise that
the gentlemen turned their horses' heads to see whether
any one was taken ill. When they heard what was the
matter, persecution began for us both.

We used to compare our experiences; the ladies
trying to persuade me now that it was improper, now that
I should be terrified to death, now that I should become
too ugly to be presentable; while the gentlemen made
game of M. de Bellaise as a foolish young lover, who was
so absurd as to encumber himself with a wife of whom
he would soon weary, and whose presence would interfere
with his enjoyment of the freedom and diversions of
military life. He who was only just free from his
governor, would he saddle himself with a wife? Bah!

He who had been so shy defended himself with
spirit; and on my side I declared that nothing but

his commands, and those of my father, should induce me to leave him. At Amiens we met a courier on his way to England, and by him we despatched letters to my father.

M. de Nidemerle treated all like absurd childish nonsense, complimenting me ironically all the while; but I thought he wavered a little' before the journey was over, wishing perhaps that he had never given his nephew a strange, headstrong, English wife, but thinking that, as the deed was done, the farther off from himself she was the better.

At least, he no longer blamed his nephew and threatened him with his aunt; but declared that Madame de Rambouillet would soon put all such folly out of our minds.

I asked my husband what Madame de Rambouillet could have to do with our affairs; and he shrugged his shoulders and answered that the divine Arthenice was the supreme judge of decorum, whose decisions no one could gainsay.

CHAPTER IV.

THE SALON BLEU.

WE arrived at Paris late in the day, entering the city through a great fortified gateway, and then rolling slowly through the rough and narrow streets. You know them too well, my children, to be able to conceive how strange and new they seemed to me, accustomed as I was to our smooth broad Thames and the large gardens of the houses in the Strand lying on its banks.

Our carriage turned in under the *porte cochère* of this Hôtel de Nidemerle of ours, and entered the courtyard. My husband, his uncle, and I know not how many more, were already on the steps. M. de Nidemerle solemnly embraced me and bade me welcome, presenting me at the same time to a gentleman, in crimson velvet and silver, as my brother. My foolish heart bounded for a moment as if it could have been Eustace; but it was altogether the face of a stranger, except for a certain fine smile like my mother's. It was, of course, my half-brother, M. le Baron de Solivet, who saluted me, and politely declared himself glad to make the acquaintance of his sister.

The Marquis then led me up the broad stairs, lined with lackeys, to our own suite of apartments, where I was to arrange my dress before being presented to Madame de Nidemerle, who begged me to excuse her not being present to greet me, as she had caught cold and had a frightful megrim.

I made my toilet, and they brought me a cup of *eau sucrée* and a few small cakes, not half enough for my hungry English appetite.

My husband looked me over more anxiously than ever he had done before; and I wished, for his sake, that I had been prettier and fitter to make a figure among all these grand French ladies.

My height was a great trouble to me in those un-formed days. I had so much more length to dispose of than my neighbours, and I knew they remarked me the more for it; and then my hair never would remain in curl for half an hour together. My mother could put it up safely, but since I had left her it was always coming down, like flax from a distaff; and though I had in general a tolerably fresh and rosy complexion, heat outside and agitation within made my whole face, nose and all, instantly become the colour of a clove gillyflower. It had so become every afternoon on the journey, and I knew I was growing redder and redder every moment, and that I should put him, my own dear Viscount, to shame before his aunt.

"Oh! my friend," I sighed, "pardon me, I cannot help it."

"Why should I pardon thee?" he answered tenderly. "Because thou hast so great and loving a heart?"

"Ah! but what will thine aunt think of me?"

"Let her think," he said. "Thou art mine, not Madame's."

I know not whether those words made me less red, but they gave me such joyous courage that I could have confronted all the dragoons, had I been of the colour of a boiled lobster, and when he himself sprinkled me for the last time with essences, I felt ready to defy the censure of all the marchionesses in France.

My husband took me by the hand and led me to the great chamber, where in an alcove stood the state bed, with green damask hangings fringed with gold, and in the midst of pillows trimmed with point-lace sat up Madame la Marquise, her little sallow face, like a bit of old parchment, in the midst of the snowy linen, and not —to my eyes—wearing a very friendly aspect.

She had perhaps been hearing of my wilfulness and insubordination, for she was very grand and formal with me, solemnly calling me Madame la Vicomtesse, and never her niece, and I thought all the time that I detected a sneer. If I had wished for my husband's sake to accom-

pany him, I wished it ten thousand times more when I
fully beheld the alternative.

Ah! I am writing treason. Had I been a well-
trained French young girl I should have accepted my
lot naturally, and no doubt all the family infinitely
regretted that their choice had fallen on one so impractic-
able.

I was happier at the supper-table, to which we were
soon summoned, for I had become accustomed to M. de
Nidemerle, who was always kind to me. Poor old man,
I think he had hoped to have something young and lively
in his house; but I never thought of that, and of course
my husband was my only idea.

M. de Solivet sat by me, and asked many questions
about my mother and the rest of the family, treating me
more as a woman than any one else had done. Nor
was it long before I caught slight resemblances both to
my mother and to my brother Berenger, which made me
feel at home with him. He was a widower, and his two
daughters were being educated in a convent, where he
promised to take me to visit them, that I might describe
them to their grandmother.

Poor little things! I thought them very stiff and
formal, and pitied them when I saw them; but I believe
they were really full of fun and frolic among their companions.

M. de Solivet was consulted on this wild scheme of

mine, and the Marchioness desired him to show me its
absurdity.   He began by arguing that it was never well
to act in the face of custom, and that he had only known
of two ladies who had followed their husbands to the
wars, and both of them only belonged to the *petite noblesse*,
and were no precedent for me! One of them had
actually joined her husband when wounded and made
prisoner, and it was said that her care had saved his
life!

Such a confession on his part rendered me the more
determined, and we reminded M. de Nidemerle of his
promise to consult Madame de Rambouillet, though I
would not engage even then to abide by any decision
except my father's, which I daily expected.   I overheard
people saying how much M. de Bellaise was improved by
his marriage, and how much more manly and less em-
barrassed he had become, and I felt that my resolution
made him happy, so that I became the more determined.

Children, you who have laughed at *Les Précieuses* can
have little idea what the Hôtel de Rambouillet was
when, three nights after my arrival, I went thither with
my husband and his uncle and aunt.

The large *salon*, hung and draped with blue velvet,
divided by lines of gold, was full of people ranged in a
circle, listening eagerly to the recital of a poem by the
author, an Abbé, who stood in the midst, declaiming each
couplet with emphasis, and keeping time with his foot,

while he made gestures with his uplifted hand. Indeed, I thought at first he was in a furious passion and was going to knock some one down, till I saw how calmly every one sat; and then again I fancied we had come to a theatre by mistake; but happily I did not speak, and, without interrupting the declamation, chairs were given us, and exchanging a mute salutation with a lady of a noble cast of beauty, who guided us to seats, we quietly took our places. She was Julie d'Argennes, the daughter of Madame de Rambouillet. A gentleman followed her closely, the Duke of Montausier, who adored her, but whom she could not yet decide on accepting.

I found it difficult to keep from laughing at the gestures of the Abbé, especially when I thought of my brothers and how they would mock them; but I knew that this would be unpardonable bad taste, and as I had come in too late to have the clue to the discourse, I amused myself with looking about me.

Perhaps the most striking figure was that of the hostess, with her stately figure, and face, not only full of intellect, but of something that went far beyond it, and came out of some other higher world, to which she was trying to raise this one.

Next I observed a lady, no longer in her first youth, but still wonderfully fair and graceful. She was en-throned in a large arm-chair, and on a stool beside her sat her daughter, a girl of my own age, the most lovely creature I had ever seen, with a profusion of light flaxen hair, and deep blue eyes, and one moment full of grave thought, at another of merry mischief. A youth sat by, whose cast of features reminded me of the Prince of Wales, but his nose was more aquiline, his dark blue eyes far more intensely bright and flashing, and whereas Prince Charles would have made fun of all the flourishes of our poet, they seemed to inspire in this youth an ardour he could barely restrain, and when there was something vehement about *Mon epée et ma patrie* he laid his hand on his sword, and his eyes lit up, so that he reminded me of a young eagle.

This was the Princess of Condé, who in the pride of her youthful beauty had been the last flame of Henri IV., who had almost begun a war on her account; this was her lovely daughter, Mademoiselle de Bourbon, and her sons, the brave Duke of Enghien, with his deformed brother, the Prince of Conti.

When the recital was over, there was a general outburst of applause, in which M. de Nidemerle joined heartily. Madame de Rambouillet gave her meed of approbation, but her daughter, Mademoiselle d'Argennes, took exception at the use of the word *chevaucher*, for to ride, both as being obsolete, and being formed from the name of a single animal, instead of regularly derived from a Latin verb.

The Abbé defended his word, and for fully twenty

minutes there was an eager argument, people citing
passages and derivations, and defining shades of meaning
with immense animation and brilliant wit, as I now
understand, though then it seemed to me a wearisome
imbroglio about a trifle. I did not know what real
benefit was done by these discussions in purifying the
language from much that was coarse and unrefined.
Yes, and far more than the language, for Madame de
Rambouillet, using her great gifts as a holy trust for the
good of her neighbour, conferred no small benefit on her
generation, nor is that good even yet entirely vanished.
Ah! if there were more women like her, France and
society would be very different.

When the discussion was subsiding, Mademoiselle
d'Argennes came to take me by the hand, and to present
us to the queen of the *salon*.

"Here, my mother, are our Odoardo and Gildippe,"
she said.

You remember, my children, that Odoardo and Gildippe are the names bestowed by Tasso on the English
married pair who went together on the first crusade, and
Gildippe continued to be my name in that circle, my
nom de Parnasse, as it was called—nay, Madame de
Montausier still gives it to me.

The allusion was a fortunate one; it established a
precedent, and, besides, English people have always been
supposed to be eccentric. I am, however, doing the

noble lady injustice. Arthenice, as she was called by an
anagram of her baptismal name of Catherine, was no
blind slave to the conventional. She had originality
enough to have been able to purify the whole sphere in
which she moved, and to raise the commonplace into
the ideal. "Excuse me," she said to her friends, and
she led my husband apart into a deep window, and there,
as he told me, seemed to look him through and through.
And verily he was one who needed not to fear such an
inspection, any more than the clearest crystal.

Then, in like manner, she called for me, and made
me understand that I was condemning myself to a life
of much isolation, and that I must be most circumspect
in my conduct, while, after all, I might see very little of
my husband; I must take good care that my presence
was a help and refreshment, not a burden and perplexity
to him, or he would neglect me and repent my coming.
"It may seem strange," she said, "but I think my young
friend will understand me, that I have always found
that, next of course to those supplied by our holy religion,
the best mode of rendering our life and its inconveniences
endurable is to give them a colouring of romance." I
did not understand her then, but I have often since
thought of her words, when the recollection of the poeti-
cal aspect of the situation has aided my courage and my
good temper. Madame de Rambouillet looked into my
eyes as she spoke, then said : " Pardon an old woman, my

dear;" and kissed my brow, saying: "You will do what I have only dreamt of."

Finally she led us forward to our great-uncle, saying: "M. le Marquis, I have conversed with these children. They love one another, and so long as that love lasts they will be better guardians to one another than ten governors or twenty *dames de compagnie.*"

In England we should certainly not have done all this in public, and my husband and I were terribly put to the blush; indeed, I felt my whole head and neck burning, and caught a glimpse of myself in a dreadful mirror, my white bridal dress and flaxen hair making my fiery face look, my brothers would have said, " as if I had been skinned."

And then, to make it all worse, a comical little crooked lady, with a keen lively face, came hopping up with hands outspread, crying: " Ah, let me see her! Where is the fair Gildippe, the true heroine, who is about to confront the arrows of the Lydians for the sake of the lord of her heart?"

" My niece," said the Marquis, evidently gratified by the sensation I had created, " Mademoiselle de Scudery does you the honour of requesting to be presented to you."

I made a low reverence, terribly abashed, and I fear it would have reduced my mother to despair, but it was an honour that I appreciated; for now that I was a

married woman, I was permitted to read romances, and I
had just begun on the first volume of the *Grand Cyrus*.
My husband read it to me as I worked at my embroidery,
and you may guess how we enjoyed it.

But I had no power of making compliments,—nay, my
English heart recoiled in anger at their making such an
outcry, whether of blame or praise, at what seemed to me
the simplest thing in the world. The courtesy and consideration were perfect; as soon as these people saw that
I was really abashed and distressed, they turned their
attention from me. My husband was in the meantime
called to be presented to the Duke of Enghien, and I remained for a little while unmolested, so that I could
recover myself a little. Presently a soft voice close to
me said " Madame," and I looked up into the beautiful
countenance of Anne Geneviève de Bourbon, her blue eyes
shining on me with the sweetest expression. " Madame,"
she said, " permit me to tell you how glad I am for you."

I thanked her most heartily. I felt this was the real
tender sympathy of a being of my own age and like myself, and there was something so pathetic in her expression that I felt sorry for her.

" You are good ! You will keep good," she said.

" I hope so, Mademoiselle," I said.

" Ah ! yes, you will. They will not make you lose
your soul against your will ! " and she clenched her delicate white hand.

" Nobody can do that, Mademoiselle."

" What! Not when they drag you to balls and *fêtes* away from the cloister, where alone you can be safe ?"

" I hope not there alone," I said.

" For me it is the only place," she repeated. " What is the use of wearing haircloth when the fire of the Bourbons is in one's blood, and one has a face that all the world runs after ? "

" *Mais*, Mademoiselle," I said ; " temptation is only to prove our strength."

" You are strong. You have conquered," she said, and clasped my hand. " But then you loved him."

I suppose I smiled a little with my conscious bliss, for this strange young princess hastily asked : " Did you love him ? I mean, before you were married."

" Oh no," I said, glad to disavow what was so shocking in my new country.

" But he is lovable ? Ah! that is it. While you are praying to Heaven, and devoting yourself to a husband whom you love, remember that if I ruin my soul, it is because they would have it so !"

At that moment there was a pause. A gentleman, the Marquis de Feuquières, had come in, bringing with him a very young lad, in the plain black gown and white collar of a theological student ; and it was made known that the Marquis had been boasting of the wonderful facility of a youth who was studying at the College of Navarre, and had declared that he could extemporise with eloquence upon any subject. Some one had begged that the youth might be fetched and set to preach on a text proposed to him at the moment, and here he was.

Madame de Rambouillet hesitated a little at the irreverence, but the Duke of Enghien requested that the sermon might take place, and she consented, only looking at her watch and saying it was near midnight, so that the time was short. M. Voiture, the poet, carried round a velvet bag, and each was to write a text on a slip of paper to be drawn out at haphazard.

We two showed each other what we wrote. My husband's was—" Love is strong as death; " mine— " Let the wife cleave unto her husband." But neither of them was drawn out. I saw by the start that Mademoiselle de Bourbon gave that it was hers, when the first paper was taken out—" Vanity of vanities, all is vanity !" A few minutes were offered to the young Abbé to collect his thoughts, but he declined them, and he was led to a sort of a daïs at the end of the *salon*, while the chairs were placed in a half-circle. Some of the ladies tittered a little, though Madame de Rambouillet looked grave ; but they composed themselves. We all stood and repeated the *Ave*, and then seated ourselves ; while the youth, in a voice already full and sweet, began solemnly : " What is life ? what is man ?"

I can never convey to you how this world and all its fleeting follies seemed to melt away before us, and how each of us felt our soul alone in the presence of our Maker, as though nothing mattered, or ever would matter, but how we stood with Him.   One hardly dared to draw one's breath.   Mademoiselle de Bourbon was almost stifled with the sobs she tried to restrain lest her mother should make her retire.   My husband held my hand, and pressed it unseen.   He was a deeper, more thoughtful man ever after he heard that voice, which seemed to come, as it were, from the Angel at Bochim who warned the Israelites; and that night we dedicated ourselves to the God who had not let us be put asunder.

I wished we could have gone away at once and heard no more, and so must, I think, the young preacher have felt; but he was surrounded with compliments.   M. Voiture said he had never heard "so early nor so late a sermon;" while others thronged up with their compliments.

Madame de Rambouillet herself murmured: "He might be Daniel hearing the compliments of Belshazzar on his deciphering the handwriting," so impassively did he listen to the suffrages of the assembly, only replying by a bow.

The Duke of Enghien, boldest of course, pressed up to him and, taking his hand, begged to know his name.

"Bossuet, Monseigneur," he answered.

There were one or two who had the bad taste to smile, for Bossuet (I must tell my English kindred) means a draught-ox; but once more the lovely sister of the young Duke grasped my hand and said : " Oh, that I could hide myself at once! Why will they not let me give myself to my God? Vanity of vanities! why am I doomed ? "

I was somewhat frightened, and was glad that a summons of " my daughter " from the Princess of Condé interrupted these strange communications. I understood them better when we were called upon to tell the old Marchioness the names of every one whom we had met at the Hôtel de Rambouillet, and on hearing of the presence of Mademoiselle de Bourbon she said: " Ah! yes, a marriage is arranged for the young lady with the Duke of Longueville."

" But ! " exclaimed my husband, " the Duke is an old man, whose daughter is older than I."

" What has that to do with it ? " said his aunt. " There is not much blood in France with which a Montmorency Bourbon can match. Moreover, they say the child is *dévote*, and *entêtée* on Madame de Port Royal, who is more than suspected of being *outrée* in her devotion ; so the sooner she is married the better !"

Poor beautiful girl, how I pitied her then! Her lovely, wistful, blue eyes haunted me all night, in the midst of my own gladness; for a courier had come that evening bringing my father's reply.   He said my mother deplored my unusual course, but that for his part he liked his little girl the better for her courage, and that he preferred that I should make my husband's home happy to my making it at court.   All he asked of me was to remember that I had to guard the honour of my husband's name and of my country, and he desired that I should take Tryphena with me wherever I went.

CHAPTER V.

IN GARRISON.

I AM almost afraid to dwell on those happiest days of my life that I spent in garrison. My eyes, old as they are, fill with tears when I am about to write of them, and yet they passed without my knowing how happy they were; for much of my time was spent in solitude, much in waiting, much in anxiety; but ah! there then always was a possibility that never, never can return!

Nancy seems to me a paradise when I look back to it, with its broad clean streets and open squares, and the low houses with balconies, and yet there I often thought myself miserable, for I began to learn what it was to be a soldier's wife. Madame de Rambouillet had kindly written to some of her friends in the duchy of Lorraine respecting me, and they assisted us in obtaining a lodging and servants. This might otherwise have been difficult, for the Duke was in the Spanish army, while we held his territories, and naturally we were not in very good odour with the people.

My husband had to leave me, immediately after he had
placed me in my little house at Nancy, to join the army
in Germany under Marshal Guêbrian. I lived through
that time by the help of the morning mass, of needlework,
and of the *Grand Cyrus*, which I read through and then
began again. My dear husband never failed to send me
a courier once a week with letters that were life to me,
and sometimes I heard from England; but my mother's
letters were becoming full of anxiety, affairs were looking
so ill for the king.

After a gallant victory over the Swedes my Viscount
returned to me without a wound, and with distinguished
praise from the Marshal. That was an important winter,
for it saw the deaths of the great Cardinal and of King Louis
XIII., moreover of the old Marchioness. My husband's
loving heart sorrowed for her and for his uncle; but that
same week brought thee to my arms, my dear son, my
beloved Gaspard! Oh, what a fight Tryphena and I had
to prevent his being stifled in swaddling clothes! And
how all the women predicted that his little limbs would
be broken and never be straight.

That winter was only clouded by the knowledge that
spring would take my husband away again. How good
he was to me! How much pleasure and amusement he
gave up for my sake! He had outgrown his bashfulness
and embarrassment in this campaign, and could take his
place in company, but he remained at home with me.

I had neither the grace nor the vivacity that would have enabled me to collect a society around me, and I seldom saw his brother officers except my brother M. de Solivet, and his great friend M. de Chamillard, who was quite fatherly to me.

The Duke of Enghien took the command of the army of Picardy, and asked for our regiment. I entreated not to be sent back to Paris, and prevailed to be allowed to take up my abode at Mezières, where I was not so far from the camp but that my dear M. de Bellaise could sometimes ride over and see me. He told me of the murmur of the elder men of the army that the fiery young inexperienced prince was disregarding all the checks that the old Marshal de l'Hôpital put in his way; but he himself was delighted, and made sure of success. The last time he came he told me he heard that Rocroy was invested by the enemy. I was made to promise that in case of any advance on the enemy's part I would instantly set off for Paris. He said it was the only way to make him fight with a free heart, if a battle there were, and not repent of having permitted me to follow him, and that I must think of my child as well as myself; but he did not expect any such good fortune as a battle, the old marshal was so set against it!

But I knew that he did expect a battle, by the way he came back and back again to embrace me and his child.

I have waited and watched many times since that day, but never as I then waited. With what agony I watched and prayed! how I lived either before the altar, or at the window! how I seemed to be all eyes and ears! How reports came that there was fighting, then that we had the day, then that all was lost! Then came a calm, and it was said that Marshal de l'Hôpital had refused to fight, and was in full retreat, with the Duke of Enghien cursing and swearing and tearing his hair. My landlord had a visit from the mayor to say that he must prepare to have some men billeted on him, and I sent out to inquire for horses, but decided that, as it was only our own troops retreating, there would be plenty of time. Then one of the maids of the house rushed in declaring that firing was plainly to be heard. Half the people were out in the streets, many more had gone outside the city to listen. Tryphena sat crying with fright, and rocking the baby in her lap, and wishing she had never come to this dreadful country. Alas! poor Tryphena, she would have been no better off in her own at that moment! I ran from window to door, unable to rest a moment, listening to the cries in the streets, asking the landlady what she heard, and then running back to my own room to kneel in prayer, but starting up at the next sound in the streets.

At last, just before sunset, on that long, long 19th of May, all the bells began to ring, clashing as if mad with joy, and a great roaring shout burst out all over the city: "Victory! Victory! Vive le Roi! Vive le Duc d'Enghien!"

I was at the window just in time to see a party of splendid horsemen, carrying the striped and castellated colours of Spain, galloping through the town, followed by universal shouts and acclamations. My man-servant, Nicole, frantic with joy, came in to tell me that they had only halted at the inn long enough to obtain fresh horses, on their way to the Queen-Regent with the news of the great victory of Rocroy. More standards taken, more cannon gained, more of the enemy killed and captive than could be counted, and all owing to the surpassing valour of the Duke of Enghien!

"And my husband!" I cried, and asked everybody, as if, poor little fool that I was, any one was likely to know how it fared with one single captain of the dragoons of Condé on such a day as that!

The good landlady and Tryphena both tried to reassure me that if there were ill news it would have been sent to me at once; but though they persuaded me at last to go to bed, I could not sleep, tossing about and listening till morning light, when I dropped into a sound sleep, which lasted for hours. I had longed for the first morning mass to go and pray there, but after all I only heard the bells through my slumber, feeling as if I could not rouse myself, and then—as it seemed to me, in another

moment—I heard something that made me turn round
on my pillow and open my eyes, and there he stood—my
husband himself. His regiment had surpassed itself;
he had received the thanks of his colonel; he had but
snatched a few hours' sleep, and had ridden off to assure
his Gildippe of his safety by her own eyes, and to rejoice
over our splendid victory.

And yet he could not but shudder as he spoke.
When they had asked a Spanish prisoner how many
there had been in the army, " Count the dead," he
proudly answered. Nor could my husband abstain from
tears as he told me how the old Spanish guards were all
lying as they stood, slain all together, with their colonel,
the Count of Fontanès, at their head, sitting in the arm-
chair in which he had been carried to the field, for he
was more than eighty years old, and could not stand or
ride on account of the gout.

The Duke of Enghien had said that if he had not
been victorious, the next best thing would be to have
died like that.

But his charges, his fire, his coolness, his skill, the
vehemence which had triumphed over the caution of the
old marshal, and the resolution which had retrieved the
day when his colleague was wounded; of all this M. de
Bellaise spoke with passionate ardour and enthusiasm,
and I—oh! I think that was the happiest and most
glorious day of all my life!

When we went together to mass, how everybody
looked at him! and when we returned there was quite a
little crowd—M. le Gouverneur and his officials eager to
make their compliments to M. de Bellaise, and to ask
questions about the Duke and about the battle, and
whether he thought the Duke would march this way, in
which case a triumphal entry should be prepared. They
wanted to have regaled M. de Bellaise with a banquet,
and were sadly disappointed when he said he had only
stolen a few hours to set his wife's heart at rest, and must
return immediately to the camp.

There was little after that to make me anxious, for
our army merely went through a course of triumphs,
taking one city after another in rapid succession. I remained at Mezières, and M. de Bellaise sometimes was
able to spend a few days with me, much, I fear, to the
derision of his fellow-soldiers, who could not understand
a man's choosing such a form of recreation. We had been
walking under the fine trees in the *Place* on a beautiful
summer evening, and were mounting the stairs on our
return home, when we heard a voice demanding of the
hostess whether this were the lodging of Captain de Bellaise.

I feared that it was a summons from the camp, but
as the stranger came forward I saw that he was a very
young man in the dress of a groom, booted, spurred, and
covered with dust and dried splashes of mud, though his
voice and pronunciation were those of a gentleman.

"Do you bring tidings from M. le Marquis?" inquired my husband, who had recognised our livery.

"Ah! I have deceived you likewise, and no wonder, for I should not have known you, Philippe," cried the new comer.

"Armand d'Aubépine! Impossible! I thought your child was a girl," exclaimed my husband.

"And am I to waste my life and grow old ingloriously on that account?" demanded the youth, who had by this time come up to our rooms.

"Welcome, then, my brother," said my husband, a little gravely, as I thought. "My love," he added, turning to me, "let me present to you my brother-in-law, the Chevalier d'Aubépine."

With infinite grace the Chevalier put a knee to the ground, and kissed my hand.

"Madame will be good enough to excuse my present appearance," he said, "in consideration of its being the only means by which I could put myself on the path of honour."

"It is then an evasion?" said my husband gravely.

"My dear Viscount, do not give yourself the airs of a patriarch. They do not suit with your one-and-twenty years, even though you are the model of husbands. Tell me, where is your hero?"

"The Duke? He is before Thionville."

"I shall be at his feet in another day. Tell me how goes the war. What cities are falling before our arms?"

UNIVERSITY OF
ILLINOIS LIBRARY

He asked of victories ; M. de Bellaise asked of his
sister. " Oh ! well, well, what do I know ? " he answered
lightly, as if the matter were beneath his consideration ;
and when I inquired about his child, he actually made a
grimace, and indeed he had barely seen her, for she had
been sent out to be nursed at a farmhouse, and he did
not even recollect her name. I shall never forget how
he stared, when at the sound of a little cry my husband
opened the door and appeared with our little Gaspard,
now five months old, laughing and springing in his arms,
and feeling for the gold on his uniform. The count
had much the same expression with which I have seen
a lady regard me when I took a caterpillar in my
hand.

" Ah ! ah !" cried our Chevalier ; " with all his legs
and arms too ! That is what comes of marrying an
Englishwoman." [He did not know I was within hearing, for I had gone in to give Tryphena orders about the
room he would occupy.] " Besides, it is a son."

" I hope one day to have a daughter whom I shall
love the more, the more she resembles her mother," said
my husband, to tease him.

" Bah ! You will not have to detest her for keeping
you back from glory ! Tell me, Philippe, could a *lettre
de cachet* reach me here ?"

" We are on French soil. What have you been
doing, Armand ?"

"Only flying from inglorious dulness, my friend. Do not be scandalised, but let me know how soon I can reach the hero of France, and enrol myself as a volunteer."

"The Duke is at Binche. I must return thither to-morrow. You had better eat and sleep here to-night, and then we can decide what is to be done."

"I may do that," the youth said, considering. "My grandfather could hardly obtain an order instantaneously, and I have a fair start."

So M. de Bellaise lent him some clothes, and he appeared at supper as a handsome lively-looking youth, hardly come to his full height, for he was only seventeen, with a haughty bearing, and large, almost fierce dark eyes, under eyebrows that nearly met.

At supper he told us his story. He was, as you know, the only scion of the old house of Aubépine, his father having been killed in a duel, and his mother dying at his birth. His grandparents bred him up with the most assiduous care, but (as my husband told me) it was the care of pride rather than of love. When still a mere boy, they married him to poor little Cécile de Bellaise, younger still, and fresh from her convent, promising, on his vehement entreaty, that so soon as the succession should be secured by the birth of a son, he should join the army.

Imagine then his indignation and despair when a little

daughter—a miserable little girl, as he said—made her appearance, to prolong his captivity. For some centuries, he said—weeks he meant—he endured, but then came the tidings of Rocroy to drive him wild with impatience, and the report that there were negotiations for peace completed the work. He made his wife give him her jewels and assist his escape from the window of her chamber; bribed a courier—who was being sent from M. de Nidemerle to my husband—to give him his livery and passport and despatches, and to keep out of sight; and thus passed successfully through Paris, and had, through a course of adventures which he narrated with great spirit, safely reached us. Even if the rogue of a courier, as he justly called his accomplice, had betrayed him, there was no fear but that he would have time to put himself on the roll of the army, whence a promising young noble volunteer was not likely to be rejected.

My husband insisted that he should write to ask the pardon of his grandfather, and on that condition engaged to introduce him to the Duke and to the lieutenant-colonel of his regiment. M. de Bellaise then inquired anxiously after the health of our uncle, who, on the death of his wife, had retired to his own estate at Nid de Merle, close to the Château d'Aubépine. Of this the young gentleman could tell little or nothing.

" Bah !" he said, adding what he thought was a brilliant new military affirmation, unaware that it was as old as the days of the League. " What know I ? He is, as all old men are, full of complaints."

Handsome, graceful, courteous, spirited as was this young Chevalier, I could not like him, and I afterwards told my husband that I wondered at his assisting him.

" My love," he said, " the Château d'Aubépine is dull enough to die of. The poor fellow was eating out his own heart. He has followed his instinct, and it is the only thing that can save him from worse corruption."

" His instinct of selfishness," I said. " His talk was all of glory, but it was of his own glory, not his duty nor the good of his country. He seems to me to have absolutely no heart !"

" Do not be hard on him ; remember how he has been brought up."

" You were brought up in like manner by two old people."

" Ah ! but they loved me. Besides, my tutor and his were as different as light and darkness."

" And your poor little sister," I said.

" She must have won his gratitude by her assistance. He will have learnt to love her when he returns. Come, *ma mie*, you must forgive him. If you knew what his captivity was, you could not help it. He was the play-fellow of my boyhood, and if I can help him to the more noble path, my aid must not be wanting, either for his sake or that of my sister."

How wise and how noble these two years had made my dear husband; how unlike the raw lad I had met at Whitehall! It was the training in self-discipline that he had given himself for my sake—yes, and for that of his country and his God.

CHAPTER VI.

VICTORY DEARLY BOUGHT.

No difficulty was made about enrolling the Chevalier d'Aubépine as a volunteer in the regiment of Condé, and as to the *lettre de cachet*, as my brother De Solivet said, the Cardinal understood his game too well to send one to bring back a youth who had rushed to place himself beneath the banners of his country in the hands of a prince of the blood.

Indeed, we soon learned that there was no one to pursue him. His grandfather had a stroke of apoplexy in his rage on hearing of the arrest, and did not survive it a week, so that he had become Count of Aubépine. The same courier brought to my husband a letter from his sister, which I thought very stiff and formal, all except the conclusion: "Oh, my brother, I implore you on my knees to watch over him and bring him back to me!"

Yet, as far as we knew and believed, the young man had never written at all to his poor little wife. My husband had insisted on his producing a letter to his grandfather; but as to his wife, he shrugged his shoulders, said that she could see that he was safe, and that was enough for her.

He was, in fact, like one intoxicated with the delights of liberty and companionship. He enjoyed a certain *éclat* from the manner of his coming, and was soon a universal favourite among the officers. Unfortunately, the influence and example there were not such as to lead him to think more of his wife. The Duke of Enghien had been married against his will to a poor little childish creature, niece to Cardinal de Richelieu, and he made it the fashion to parade, not only neglect, but contempt, of one's wife. He was the especial hero of our young Count's adoration, and therefore it was the less wonder that, when in the course of the winter the chaplain wrote that the young Madame la Comtesse was in the most imminent danger, after having given birth to the long-desired son and heir, he treated the news with supreme carelessness. We should never have known whether she lived or died, had not the courier, by whom M. de Bellaise wrote to her as well as to his uncle, brought back one of her formal little letters, ill-spelt and un-meaning, thanking *Monsieur son frère* and *Madame sa femme* for their goodness, and saying she was nearly recovered.

" It cuts me to the heart to receive such letters," said my husband, " and to feel how little I can be to her.

Some day I hope I may know her better, and make her feel what a brother means."

All this happened while we were in garrison for the winter at Nancy. Again we offered M. d'Aubépine a room in our house; but though he was, in his way, fond of my husband, and was polite to me, he thought a residence with us would interfere with his liberty, and, alas! his liberty consisted in plunging deeper and deeper into dissipation, gambling, and all those other sports which those about him made him think the privileges of manhood. We could do nothing; he laughed at M. de Bellaise, and so indeed did these chosen friends of his. I believe plenty of wit was expended on us and our happy domestic life; but what was that to us? The courage of M. de Bellaise was well known, and he had so much good-temper and kindness that no one durst insult him.

He was doubly tender to me that winter and spring because the accounts from England were so sad. My dear brother Berenger had been killed at the battle of Alresford, and affairs looked very ill for the royal cause. I wept for my brother; but, ah! those tears were as nothing compared with what I was soon to shed.

The Duke of Enghien arrived. He was not to take the command of the army of the Low Countries, but of that of Germany. He came on the very day we had heard of the loss of Freiburg in Brisgau, and all was at once activity. I saw the inspection of the army just outside the city, and a glorious sight it was; bodies of infantry moving like one great machine, squadrons of cavalry looking invincible, all glittering with gold, and their plumes waving, the blue and gold banners above their heads; and the dear regiment of Condé, whence salutes from eye and hand came to me and my little Gaspard as they rode past.

I did not tremble as in the last campaign. Ah! perhaps I did not pray so much. I heard of the crossing of the Rhine at Brisach, and then came rumours of a tremendous battle at Freiburg. The bells had only just begun to ring, when Pierre, our groom, galloped into the town, and sent up at once his packet. His master, he said, was wounded, but not badly, and had covered himself with glory. I tore open the packet. There were a few lines by his own dear hand:—

"MY HEART—I shall be with thee soon to rest in thy care.—D. G. Kiss our son. Thy B."

The rest of the packet was from my half-brother De Solivet, and told how, in the frightful attack on the vineyard at Freiburg, seven times renewed, my dear, dear Philippe had received a shot in the knee, just as he was grasping a Bavarian standard, which he carried off with him. He would have returned to the charge, but faintness overpowered him, and he was supported on horseback from the field to the tent. The wound had been dressed, and the surgeon saw no occasion for alarm. M. de Solivet, who had a slight wound himself, and M. d'Aubépine, who was quite uninjured, though he had done prodigies of valour, would tend him with all their hearts.   I had better send the carriage and horses at once to bring him back, as the number of wounded was frightful, and means of transport were wanting.   Then followed a message of express command from my husband that I was not to think of coming with the carriage.   He would not have me at Freiburg on any account.

I submitted; indeed I saw no cause for fear, and even rejoiced that for a long time I should have my husband to myself.   I made all ready for him, and taught my little Gaspard now he would say : " *Soyez le bienvenu, mon papa.*"

So passed a week.   Then one day there was a clanking of spurs on the stairs; I flew to the door and there stood M. d'Aubépine.

" Is he near ?" I cried, and then I saw he was white and trembling.

" Ah ! no," he cried ; " he is at Brisach !   We could bring him no farther.   Can you come with me, Madame ?   He asks incessantly for you, and it might—it might be that your coming may revive him."

And then this wild headstrong youth actually sank into a chair, hid his face on the table, and sobbed as if his heart would break.

I had no time for weeping then. I sent for the first physician in Nancy, and offered him any sum in the world to accompany me; I had to make almost wild efforts to procure a horse, and at last had to force one from the governor by my importunities. I collected wine and cordials, and whatever could be of service, and after his first outburst my young brother-in-law helped me in a way I can never forget. No doubt the pestiferous air caused by the horrible carnage of Freiburg had poisoned the wound. As soon as possible my husband was removed; but the mischief had been already done; the wound was in a bad state, fever had set in, and though he struggled on stage after stage, declaring that he should be well when he saw me, the agony had been such on the last day that they barely got him to Brisach, and he there became delirious, so that M. de Solivet decided on remaining with him, while the Count came on to fetch me. He had ridden ever since four o'clock in the morning, and yet was ready to set out again as soon as my preparations were complete. Oh, I can never overlook what he was to me on that journey!

Hope kept us up through that dismal country—the path of war, where instead of harvest on that August day we saw down-trodden, half-burned wheat fields, where a few wretched creatures were trying to glean a few ears of wheat. Each village we passed showed only blackened walls, save where at intervals a farmhouse had been repaired to serve as an *estafette* for couriers from the French army. The desolation of the scene seemed to impress itself on my soul, and destroy the hopes with which I had set forth; but on and on we went, till the walls of Brisach rose before us.

He was in the governor's quarters, and only at the door, I perceived that M. d'Aubépine had much doubted whether we should find him alive. However, that one consolation was mine. He knew me; he smiled again on me; he called me by all his fondest names; he said that now he could rest. For twenty-four hours we really thought that joy was working a cure. Alas! then he grew worse again, and when the pain left him, mortification had set in, and we could only send for a priest to administer the last Sacraments.

I am an old woman now, and what was then the cruellest anguish touches me with pleasure when I think how he called me his guardian angel, and thanked me for having been his shield from temptation, placing his son in my sole charge, and commending his sister and his old uncle to me—his poor little sister whose lot seemed to grieve him so much. He talked to the Count, who wept, tore his hair, and made promises, which he really then intended to execute, and which at least comforted my Philippe.

The good priest who attended him said, he had never seen anything more edifying or beautiful, and that he had never heard the confession of a military man showing a purer heart, more full of holy love, trust, and penitence. There was a great peace upon us all, as his life ebbed away, and even the Count stood silent and awestruck. They took me away at last.   I remember nothing but the priest telling me that my husband was in Paradise.

I felt as if it were all a dream, and when presently my brother came and took my hand, I cried out : " Oh, wake me ! wake me ! "   And when he burst into tears I asked what he meant.

Looking back now I can see how very kind he was to me, though I made little return, being altogether bewildered by the sudden strangeness of my first grief. Poor M. de Solivet ! he must have had a heavy charge, for Armand d'Aubépine was altogether frantic with grief, and did nothing to help him, while I could not weep, and sat like a statue, hardly knowing what they said to me.   Nay, when the tidings came that my father had been killed in the battle of Marston Moor three weeks before, I was too dull and dead to grieve.   Eustace had written to my husband in order that he might prepare me ; I opened the letter, and all that I can remember feeling was that I had no one to shield me.

I had but one wish and sense of duty at that moment, namely, to carry home those dear remains to the resting-place of his fathers in Anjou, where I hope myself to rest. It was of no use to tell me that all places would be alike

to my Philippe when we should awake on the Resurrec-
tion day. I was past reason, and was possessed with a
feeling that it would be sacrilege to leave him among the
countless unnamed graves of the wounded who, like him,
had struggled as far as Brisach to die. I fancied I should
not be able to find him, and, besides, it was an enemy's
country ! I believe opposition made me talk wildly and
terrify my brother ; at any rate, he swore to me that the
thing should be done, if only I would return to Nancy
and to my child. I fancied, most unjustly, that this was
meant to deceive me, and get me out of the way while
they buried him whom I loved so much, and I refused
to stir without the coffin.

How my brother contrived it, I do not know, but the
thing was done, and though it was but a cart that carried
the coffin to Nancy, I was pacified.

At Nancy he arranged matters more suitably. Here
M. d'Aubépine, in floods of tears, took leave of me to
return to the army, and M. de Solivet, whose wound dis-
abled him from active service, undertook to escort me
and my precious convoy to Anjou.

It was a long tedious journey, and my heart beats
with gratitude to him when I think what he undertook
for me, and how dreary it must have been for him, while
I was too dead and dull to thank him, though I hope my
love and confidence evinced my gratitude in after life.

My dearest went first in a hearse drawn by mules, as

was also my large carriage,—that which we had so joy-
ously bought together, saying it would be like a kind of
tent on our travels. I travelled in it with my child and
my women, and M. de Solivet rode with our men-servants.
Our pace was too slow for the fatigue to be too much for
him, and he always preceded me to every place where we
halted to eat, or where we lodged for the night, and had
everything ready without a thought or a word being needful from me. He always stood ready to give me his
arm to take me to hear mass before we set out each day.
The perfect calm, and the quiet moving on, began to do
me good. I felt as if the journey had always been going
on, and only wished it were endless, for when it was
over I should feel my desolation, and have no more to
do for my Philippe. But I began to respond to my poor
boy's caresses and playfulness a little more; I was not
so short and *maussade* with my women or with my good
brother, and I tried to pray at mass. My brother has
since told me that he never felt more relieved in his life
than once when he made little Gaspard bring me some
blue corn-flowers and wheat, which reminded me of my
English home, so that I began to weep so profusely, that
he carried away the poor frightened child, and left me to
Tryphena.

One afternoon at a little village there was a look of
festival; the bells were ringing, everybody was hurrying
to the church, and when we stopped at the door of the

inn my brother came to the carriage-window and said he was afraid that we should not find it easy to proceed at once, for a mission priest was holding a station, and no one seemed able to attend to anything else.

" He is a true saint ! he is just about to preach," said the landlady, who had come out with her gayest apron, her whitest cap, and all her gold chains. " Ah ! the poor lady, it would do her heart good to hear him preach ; and by that time the roast would be ready—an admirable piece of venison, sent for the occasion. There he is, the blessed man ! "

And as I had just alighted from the carriage, for our mules had made a double stage and could not go farther, I saw coming from the *presbytère* three or four priests, with the sexton and the serving boys. One of them, a spare thin man, with a little bronze crucifix in his hand, paused as he saw the hearse drawn up, clasped his hands in prayer, and then lifted them in benediction of him who lay within. I saw his face, and there was in it an indescribable heavenly sweetness and pity which made me say to my brother : " I must go and hear him."

My brother was so glad to hear me express any wish, that I believe, if I had asked to go and dance on the village green, he would almost have permitted it ; and leaving my little one to play in the garden under Tryphena's care, he gave me his arm, and we went into the church, crowded—crowded so that we could hardly find room; but my deep mourning made the good people respectfully make place for us and give us chairs.

Ah! that sermon! I cannot tell you it in detail; I only know that it gave the strongest sense of healing balm to my sore heart, and seemed in a wonderful way to lift me up into the atmosphere where my Philippe was gone, making me feel that what kept me so far— far from him was not death, nor his coffin, but my own thick husk of sin and worldliness. Much more there was, which seems now to have grown into my very soul; and by the time it was over I was weeping tears no longer bitter, and feeling nothing so much as the need to speak to that priest.

M. de Solivet promised that I should, but we had long to wait, for the saintly Abbé de Paul would not postpone the poor to the rich; nor could my grief claim the precedence, for I was not the only broken-hearted young widow in France, nor even in that little village.

I cannot be grateful enough to my brother that he put up with all the inconveniences of sleeping at this little village, that I might carry out what he thought a mere woman's enthusiastic fancy: but in truth it was everything to me. After vespers the holy man was able to give me an hour in the church, and verily it was the opening of new life to me. Since my light had been taken from me, all had been utter desolate darkness before me. He put a fresh light before me, which now, after

fifty years, I know to have been the dawn of better sunshine than even that which had brightened my youth—
and I thank my good God, who has never let me entirely
lose sight of it.

Very faint, almost disappointing, it seemed to me
then.   I came away from my interview feeling as if it
had been vain to think there could be any balm for a
crushed heart, and yet when I awoke the next morning,
and dressed myself to hear mass before resuming my
journey, it was with the sense that there I should meet
a friend and comforter.   And when I looked at my little
son, it was not only with dreary passionate pity for the
unconscious orphan, but with a growing purpose to bring
him up as his father's special charge,—nay, as that from
even a greater and nearer than my Philippe.

While, as we journeyed on, I gradually dwelt less on
how piteous my arrival would be for myself, and thought
more and more of its sadness for the poor old Marquis
who had loved his nephew so much, till, instead of
merely fearing to reach Nid de Merle, I began to look forward to it, and consider how to comfort the poor old
man ; for had not my husband begged me to be the staff
of his old age, and to fill a daughter's place to him ?

CHAPTER VII.

WIDOW AND WIFE.

WE had avoided Paris, coming through Troyes and
Orleans, and thus our sad strange journey lasted a full
month.   Poor old M. de Nidemerle had, of course, been
prepared for our coming, and he came out in his coach to
meet us at the cross-roads.   My brother saw the mourning liveries approaching, and gave me notice.   I descended
from my carriage, intending to go to him in his, but
he anticipated me; and there, in the middle of the road,
the poor old man embraced me, weeping floods of passionate tears of grief.   He was a small man, shrunk with
age, and I found him clinging to me so like a child that
I felt an almost motherly sense of protection and tenderness towards his forlorn old age; but my English shyness
was at the moment distressed at the sense of all the
servants staring at such a meeting, and I cried out: "Oh,
sir! you should not have come thus."   "What can I do,
but show all honour to the heroic wife of my dear child?"
sobbed he; and, indeed, I found afterwards that my per-

sistence in bringing home my dearest to the tombs of his forefathers had won for me boundless gratitude and honour. They took the hearse to the church of the convent at Bellaise, where its precious burthen was to rest. The obsequies, requiem, and funeral mass were to take place the next day, and in the meantime I accompanied the Marquis to the château, and we spent the evening and great part of the night in talking of him whom we had both loved so dearly, and in weeping together.

Then came the solemn and mournful day of the funeral. I was taken early to the convent, where, among the nuns behind the *grille,* I might assist at these last rites.

Thickly veiled, I looked at no one except that I curtsied my thanks to the Abbess before kneeling down by the grating looking into the choir. My grief had always been too deep for tears, and on that day I was blessed in a certain exaltation of thoughts which bore me onward amid the sweet chants to follow my Philippe, my brave, pure-hearted, loving warrior, into his rest in Paradise, and to think of the worship that he was sharing there.

So I knelt quite still, but by and by I was sensible of a terrible paroxysm of weeping from some one close to me. I could scarcely see more than a black form when I glanced round, but it seemed to me that it was sinking;

I put out my arm in support, and I found a head on my
shoulder.   I knew who it must be—my husband's poor
little sister, Madame d'Aubépine, and I held my arm
round her, with an impulse of affection, as something
that was his; but before all was over, I was sure that she
was becoming faint, and at last I only moved just in
time to receive her in my lap and arms, as she sank
down nearly, if not quite, unconscious.

I tore back the heavy veil that was suffocating her,
and saw a tiny thin white face, not half so large as my
little Gaspard's round rosy one.   Numbers of black forms
hovered about with water and essences; and one tall
figure bent to lift the poor child from me, apologising
with a tone of reproof, and declaring that Madame la
Comtesse was ashamed to inconvenience Madame.

"No," I said; "one sister could not inconvenience
another," and I felt the feeble hand stealing round my
waist, and saw a sort of smile on the thin little lips,
which brought back one look of my Philippe's.   I threw
off my own veil, and raised her in my arms so as to kiss
her, and in that embrace I did indeed gain a sister.

I did not heed the scolding and the murmuring; I
lifted her; she was very small, and light as a feather;
and I was not merely tall, but very strong, so I carried
her easily to a chamber, which one of the nuns opened
for us, and laid her on the bed.   She clung to me, and
when some one brought wine, I made her drink it, and

prayed that they would leave us to ourselves a little while.

I know now that nothing but the privileges of my position on that day would have prevailed to get that grim and terrible *dame de compagnie* out of the room. However, we were left alone, and the first thing the poor young thing did when she could speak or move, was to throw herself into my arms and cry:

"Tell me of him!"

"He sent his love. He commended you to me," I began.

"Did he? Oh, my dear hero! And how is he looking?"

So it was of her husband, not her brother, that she was thinking. It gave me a pang, and yet I could not wonder; and alas, d'Aubépine had not given me any message at all for her. However, I told her what I thought would please her—of his handsome looks, and his favour with the Duke of Enghien, and her great dark eyes began to shine under their tear-swollen lids; but before long, that terrible woman knocked at the door again to say that Madame la Comtesse's carriage was ready, and that M. le Marquis awaited Madame la Vicomtesse.

We arranged our disordered dress, and went down hand-in-hand. The Marquis and the Abbess both embraced the poor little Countess, and I assured her that we would meet again, and be much together.

"Madame la Comtesse will do herself the honour of paying her respects to Madame la Vicomtesse," said the *dame de compagnie*, "since Madame la Comtesse Douarière is confined to her room, and prays to be excused."

Therewith she swept the poor little lady off with her, much like a child in disgrace; walking behind, indeed, but as if she was driving her.

When, in the evening, I asked the Marquis who she was, and M. de Solivet added that she looked fit to be a sergeant of dragoons, the old gentleman said that she was Mademoiselle de Gringrimeau, a lady of a Huguenot family, who had, since her conversion, lived as *dame de compagnie* with the elder Madame d'Aubépine, and had regulated her household of late years.

"I congratulate myself on not belonging to that respectable household," said my brother.

M. de Nidemerle laughed, and said the good lady had brought with her a fair share of Calvinist severity. In fact, it was reported that her conversion had been stimulated by the hope that she should be endowed with her family property, and bestowed in marriage on the young d'Aubépine, the father of the present youth, and that disappointment in both these expectations had embittered her life. I was filled with pity for my poor little sister-in-law, who evidently was under her yoke; and all the more when, a day or two later, the two ladies came in great state to pay me a visit of ceremony, and I saw how pale and thin was the little Countess, and how cowed she seemed by the tall and severe duenna.

Little Gaspard was trotting about. The Marquis was delighted with the child, and already loved him passionately; and the little fellow was very good, and could amuse himself without troubling any one.

He took refuge with me from Mademoiselle de Gringrimeau; but as I held him to kiss his aunt, her eyes filled with tears; and when I asked whether her little girl could walk as well as he did, she faltered so that I was startled, fearing that the child might have died and I not have heard of it.

" She is out at nurse," at last she murmured.

" Children are best at farms," said Mademoiselle de Gringrimeau; " Madame la Comtesse Douarière is not to be incommoded." The old man held out his arms to my little boy, and said something of his being a pleasure instead of an inconvenience; but though the lady answered politely, she looked so severe that my poor child hid his face on my bosom and began to cry, by way of justifying her.

However, when she was gone, both the gentlemen agreed that the little fellow was quite right, and showed his sense, and that if they had been only two years old, they would have cried too.

That was all in my favour when I entreated M. de Nidemerle to let me have a visit from my sister-in-law,

—not a mere call of ceremony, but a stay at the château long enough for me to get acquainted with her. Not only was she the only sister of my dear Philippe, but the Marquis, her uncle, was her guardian and only near relative, so that he had a right to insist, more especially as the old Countess was imbecile and bed-ridden.

I think he felt towards me much as he would have done if he had been shut up in a room with Gaspard, ready to give me anything I begged for, provided I would not cry. He was very good to me, and I could not but be sorry for the poor, bereaved, broken old man, and try to be a daughter to him; and thus our relations were very different from what they had been on our journey to Paris together in the coach. At any rate, he pro-mised me that I should be gratified, and the day after my brother left us, he actually went over to Château d'Aubépine, and brought off his niece in the carriage with him, presenting her to me in the hall like the spoils of war. She was frightened, formal, and ceremonious all supper time, but I thought she was beginning to thaw, and was more afraid of the Marquis than of me. We played at cards all the evening, the *curé* being sent for to make up the set, and now and then I caught her great eyes looking at me wistfully; indeed, I was obliged to avoid them lest they should make me weep; for it was almost the look that my Philippe used to cast on me in those early days when we had not begun to know one another.

At last we went up to bed. The rooms were all *en suite*, and I had given her one opening into mine, telling her we would never shut the door save when she wished it. I saw her gazing earnestly at her brother's portrait and all the precious little objects consecrated to his memory, which I had arranged by my *bénitier* and crucifix, but I did not expect her first exclamation, when our woman had left us: " Ah, Madame! how happy you are !"

" I was once !" I sighed.

" Ah! but you *are* happy. You have your child, and your husband loved you."

" But your husband lives, and your children are well."

" That may be. I never see them. I have only seen my daughter twice, and my son once, since they were born. They will not let them come to the château, and they say there is no road to the farms."

" We will see to that," I said, and I made her tell me where they were ; but she knew no more of distances than I did, never going anywhere save in the great family coach. Poor child ! when I called her Cécile, she burst into tears, and said no one had called her by that name since she had left her friend Amélie in the convent, and as to calling me Marguerite, Mademoiselle de Gringrimeau would be sure to say it was *bourgeois* and ill-bred to use familiar names, but then we need never let her hear us.

I took the poor little forlorn creature to sleep with me, and then, and in the course of the next day or two, the whole sad state of things came before me.

The little Cécile de Bellaise had been carried to a convent at Angers from the farm that she could just remember. Here she had spent all the happy days of her life. The nuns were not strict, and they must have been very ignorant, for they had taught her nothing but her prayers, a little reading, some writing, very bad orthography, embroidery, and heraldry; but they were very good-natured, and had a number of *pensionnaires* who seemed to have all run wild together in the corridors and gardens, and played all sorts of tricks on the nuns. Sometimes Cécile told me some of these, and very unedifying they were,—acting ghosts in the passages, fastening up the cell doors, ringing the bells at unearthly hours, putting brushes or shoes in the beds, and the like practical jokes.

Suddenly, from the midst of these wild sports, while still a mere child under fourteen, Cécile was summoned to be married to Armand d'Aubépine, who was two years older, and was taken at once to Château d'Aubépine.

There was no more play for her; she had to sit upright embroidering under the eyes of Madame la Comtesse and of Mademoiselle de Gringrimeau; nor did she

ever go out of doors except for a turn on the terrace with
the ladies, or a drive in the great coach. Of course they
were disappointed in having such a little unformed being
on their hands, but they must have forgotten that they
had ever been young themselves, when they forced her to
conform rigidly to the life that suited them, and which
they thought the only decorous thing for a lady of any
age.

There was nothing else that was young near her except her husband, and he thought her an ugly little thing,
and avoided her as much as possible. He had expected
to be freed from his tutor on his marriage, and when he
was disappointed, he was extremely displeased, and mani-
fested his wrath by neglect of her. His governor must
have been a very different one from my dear husband's
beloved abbé, for I know that if I had been five times
as ugly and stupid as I was, my Philippe would have
tried to love me, because it was his duty—and have been
kind to me, because he could not be unkind to any one.
But the Chevalier d'Aubépine had never learnt to care
for any one's pleasure but his own ; he was angry at, and
ashamed of, the wife who had been imposed on him ; he
chafed and raged at not being permitted to join the army
and see the world ; and in the meantime he, with the
connivance of his governor, from time to time escaped at
night to Saumur, and joined in the orgies of the young
officers in garrison there.

Nevertheless, through all his neglect, Cécile loved him with a passionate, faithful adoration, surpassing all words, just as I have seen a poor dog follow faithfully a savage master who gives him nothing but blows. She never said a word of complaint to me of him. All I gathered of this was from her simple self-betrayals, or from others, or indeed what I knew of himself; but the whole sustenance of that young heart had been his few civil words at times when he could make her useful to him. I am persuaded, too, that Mademoiselle de Gringrimeau exercised her spite in keeping the two young creatures from any childish or innocent enjoyments that might have drawn them together. If etiquette were the idol of that lady, I am sure that spite flavoured the incense she burned to it.

I think, if I had been in Cécile's position, I should either have gone mad, or have died under the restraint and dreariness; but she lived on in the dull dream of half-comprehended wretchedness, and gave birth to her daughter, but without being in the least cheered, for a peasant woman was in waiting, who carried the child off while she was still too much exhausted to have even kissed it. All she obtained was universal murmuring at the sex of the poor little thing. It seemed the climax of all her crimes, which might be involuntary, but for which she was made to suffer as much as if they had been her fault.

Her husband was more displeased than any one else; above all when he heard the news of Rocroy; and then it was that he devised the scheme of running away, and in discussing it with her became more friendly than ever before. Of course it was dreadful to her that he should go to the war, but the gratification of helping him, keeping his secret, plotting with him, getting a few careless thanks and promises, carried the day, and bore her through the parting. "He really did embrace me of his own accord," said the poor young creature; and it was on that embrace that she had ever since lived, in hope that when they should meet again he might find it possible to give her a few shreds of affection.

Of course, when she was found to have been cognisant of his departure, she was in the utmost disgrace. Rage at his evasion brought on the fit of apoplexy which cost the old count his life; and the blame was so laid upon her, not only by Mademoiselle de Gringrimeau, but by Madame and by her confessor, that she almost believed herself a sort of parricide; and she had not yet completed the course of penitential exercises that had been imposed on her.

By the time—more than half a year later—her son was born, the old countess had become too childish to be gratified for more than a moment. Indeed, poor Cécile herself was so ill that she survived only by a wonder, since no one cared whether she lived or died, except her own maid, who watched over her tenderly, and gave her, when she could read it, a letter from her husband upon the joyful news. She wore that letter, such as it was, next her heart, and I never told her how my husband had absolutely stood over him while he wrote it.

So she recovered, if it can be called recovery—for her health had been shattered by all this want of the most common care and consideration; she was very weak and nervous, and suffered constantly from headache, and her looks were enough to break one's heart. I suppose nothing could have made her beautiful, but she had a strange, worn, blighted, haggard, stunted look, quite dreadful for one not yet eighteen; she was very short, and fearfully thin and pale, but out of the sad little face there looked my Philippe's eyes, and now and then his smile.

After talking till late I fell asleep, and when I woke to dress for morning mass, I found that she had not slept at all, and had a frightful headache. I bade her lie still till I came back, and she seemed hardly able to believe in such luxury. Mademoiselle said nothing but resolution was wanting to shake off a headache.

" Have you found it so ? " I asked.

" At any rate, it is better than the doses Mademoiselle gives me," she said.

" You shall try my remedy this time," I said ; and I set out for the little village church, which stood at the garden-gate, with a fixed determination that this state of things—slow torture and murder, as it seemed to me— should not go on.   If one work bequeathed to me by my dear Philippe was to take care of his uncle, another surely was to save and protect his sister.

CHAPTER VIII.

MARGUERITE TO THE RESCUE.

IT was in my favour that M. de Nidemerle had conceived a very high opinion of me, far above my deserts. My dear husband's letters had been full of enthusiasm for me. I found them all among the Marquis's papers; and his tenderness and gratitude, together with the circumstances of my return, had invested me with a kind of halo, which made me a sort of heroine in his eyes.

Besides, I did my best to make the old man's life more cheerful. I read him the *Gazette* that came once a week, I played at cards with him all the evening, and I sometimes even wrote or copied his letters on business; and, when I sat at my embroidery, he liked to come and sit near me, sometimes talking, playing with Gaspard, or dozing. He was passionately fond of Gaspard, and let the child domineer over him in a way that sometimes shocked me.

Thus he was ready to believe what I told him of his niece, and assured me I might keep her with me as long as I wished, if the Countess, her mother-in-law, would consent. The first thing we did together was that I took her to see her children. The boy was at a farm not very far off; he was seven months old, and a fine healthy infant, though not as clean as I could have wished; but then Tryphena and I had been looked on as barbarians, who would certainly be the death of Gaspard, because we washed him all over every evening, and let him use his legs and arms. Cécile was enchanted; she saw an extraordinary resemblance between her son and his father; and hugged the little swaddled form like one who had been famished.

Our search for the little Armantine was less prosperous. Cécile could not ride, nor could even walk a quarter of a mile without nearly dying of fatigue; nay, the jolting of the coach as we drove along the road would have been insupportable to her but for her longing to see her little one. We drove till it was impossible to get the coach any farther, and still the farm was only just in sight.

I jumped out and said I would bring the child to her, and I went up between the hedges with two lackeys behind me, till I came to a farmyard, where three or four children, muddy up to the very eyes, were quarrelling and playing with the water of a stagnant pool. I made my way through animals, dogs, and children, to the farm kitchen, where an old grandmother and a beggar sat

on two chairs opposite to one another, on each side of the
fire, and a young woman was busy over some raw joints
of an animal. They stared at me with open mouths,
and when I said that Madame la Comtesse d'Aubépine
was come to see her child, and was waiting in the carriage, they looked as if such a thing had never been heard
of before. The young woman began to cry—the old
woman to grumble. I think if they had dared, they
would have flown into a passion, and I was really alarmed
lest the child might be sick or even dead. I told them
impressively who I was, and demanded that they would
instantly show me the little one.

The young woman, muttering something, stepped out
and brought in her arms the very dirtiest child of the
whole group I had left in the gutter, with the whole tribe
behind her. My first impulse was to snatch it up and
carry it away to its mother, taking it home at once to
Nid de Merle ; but it squalled and kicked so violently
when I held out my arms to it, that it gave me time to
think that to carry it thus away without authority might
only bring Cécile into trouble with those who had the
mastery over her, and that to see it in such a condition
could only give her pain. I should not have objected to
the mere surface dirt of grubbing in the farmyard (shocking as it may sound to you, *Mademoiselles mes Petites
Filles*). Eustace and I had done such things at Walwyn
and been never the worse for it; but this poor little

creature had a wretched, unwholesome, neglected air about her that made me miserable, and the making her fit to be seen would evidently be a long business, such as could hardly be undertaken in the midst of the salting of a pig, which was going on.

I therefore promised the woman a crown if she would make the child tidy and bring her to Nid de Merle on the Sunday. Something was muttered about Mademoiselle having said the child was not to be constantly brought to the house to incommode Madame la Comtesse; but I made her understand that I meant Nid de Merle, and trusted that the hope of the money would be a bait.

Cécile was sorely disappointed when I returned without the child, and conjured me at once to tell her the worst, if it were indeed dead; but she let herself be pacified by the hope of seeing it on Sunday, and indeed she was half dead with fatigue from the roughness of the road.

The child was duly brought by the foster-mother, who was in the full costume of a prosperous peasant, with great gold cross and gay apron; but I was not better satisfied about the little one, though she had a cleaner face, cap, and frock. Unused to the sight of black, she would let neither of us touch her, and we could only look at her, when she sat on her nurse's knee with a cake in her hand. I was sure she was unhealthy and uncared for, her complexion and everything about her showed it,

and my Gaspard was twice her size. It was well for
the peace of the young mother that she knew so little
what a child ought to be like, and that her worst grief was
that the little Armantine would not go to her.

"And oh! they will send her straight into a convent
as soon as she is weaned, and I shall never have her with
me!" sighed Cécile.

"*On.*" *On* had done many harsh things towards my
poor little sister-in-law, and I began now to consider of
whom *on* now consisted. It seemed to me to be only
Mademoiselle de Gringrimeau acting in the name of the
doting Countess and the absent husband, and that one
resolute effort might emancipate the poor young thing.

I was still considering the matter, and rallying my
forces, when a message came from the Château l'Aube that
Madame la Douarière was dying, and Madame la Comtesse
must return instantly. I went with her; I could not let
her return alone to Mademoiselle's tender mercies, and
the Marquis approved and went with us. In fact, the two
châteaux were not two miles apart, through the lanes
and woods, though the way by the road was much
longer.

The old Countess lingered another day and then ex-
pired. Before the funeral ceremonies were over, I had
seen how Mademoiselle de Gringrimeau tyrannised over
this young sister-in-law, who was still a mere gentle child,
and was absolutely cowed by the woman. When I tried

to take her home with me, Mademoiselle had the effrontery to say that the Count himself, as well as the late dowager, had given her authority over Madame as *dame de compagnie*, and that she did not consider it *etiquette* to visit after so recent a bereavement, thus decidedly hitting at me.

However, I had made up my mind. I entreated my poor weeping Cécile to hold out yet a little longer in hope; and then I returned home to lay the whole situation before the Marquis, and to beg him to assert his authority as uncle, and formally request that she might reside under his protection while her husband was with the army—a demand which could hardly fail to be granted.

I wrote also to M. d'Aubépine, over whom I thought I had some influence, and added likewise a letter to my half-brother De Solivet, explaining the situation, and entreating him to get the young gentleman into his lodgings, and not let him out till he had written his letters, signed and sealed them!

The plan answered. In due time our courier returned, and with all we wanted in the way of letters, with one great exception, alas! any true sign of tenderness for the young wife. There was a formal letter for her, telling her to put herself and her children under the charge of her uncle and her brother's widow, leaving the charge of the château and servants to the *intendant* and to Mademoiselle de Gringrimeau. The poor child had to imbibe what her yearning heart could extract from the

conventional opening and close. I have my share of the
budget still, and here it is :—

"MADAME—You still love to play your part of beneficent
angel, and wish to take on your shoulders my *impedimenta.* Well,
be it so then ; though I have no hope that you will make thereof
(*en*) anything like yourself. Kissing your hands,
                                     "LE COMTE D'AUBÉPINE."

His whole family was thus disposed of in two letters
of the alphabet (*en*).

M. de Nidemerle received a polite request to undertake
the charge of his niece, and Mademoiselle had likewise
her orders, and I heard from my brother how he had
smiled at my commands, but had found them necessary,
for Armand d'Aubépine had been exactly like a naughty
boy forced to do a task. Not that he had the smallest
objection to his wife and children being with me—in fact,
he rather preferred it; he only hated being troubled about
the matter, wanted to go to a match at tennis, and thought
it good taste to imitate the Duke of Enghien in contempt
for the whole subject. Would he ever improve ? My
brother did not give much present hope of it, saying that
on returning to winter quarters he had found the lad
plunged all the deeper in dissipation for want of the
check that my dear husband had been able to impose on
him ; but neither M. de Solivet nor the Marquis took it
seriously, thinking it only what every youth in the army
went through, unless he were such a wonderful exception
as my dear Philippe had been.

Cécile could hardly believe that such peace and comfort were in store for her, and her tyrant looked as gloomy
as Erebus at losing her slave, but we did not care for
that; we brought her home in triumph, and a fortnight's
notice was given to the foster-mother in which to wean
Mademoiselle d'Aubépine and bring her to Nid de Merle.

That fortnight was spent by our guest in bed. As
if to justify Mademoiselle de Gringrimeau, she was no
sooner under my care than she had a sharp illness; but
Tryphena, who had been so instructed by my grandmother, Lady Walwyn, as to be more skilful than any
doctor, declared that it was in consequence of the long
disregard of health and strain of spirits, and so managed
her that, though never strong, she improved much in
health, and therewith in looks. Beautiful she could hardly
be, as the world counts beauty, but to me her sweet,
tender, wistful expression made her countenance most
lovable, and so did her gentle unmurmuring humility.
She sincerely believed that all the cruel slights she under-
went were the result of her own ugliness, stupidity, and
ignorance, and instead of blaming her husband, she merely
pitied him for being tied to her. As to granting that her
brother had been a better man than her husband, she
would have thought that high treason—the difference
was only that her dear Marguerite was so pretty, so clever,
amiable, and well taught, that she had won his heart.

In truth, I had outgrown the ungainliness of my girl-

hood, and, now that it did not matter to any one, had
become rather a handsome woman, and it was of no use
to tell her that I had been worse than she, because there
was so much more of me, when my dear young husband
gave me the whole of his honest heart.

To make herself, at least, less dull was her next
desire.   One reason why she had so seldom written was
that she knew she could not spell, and Mademoiselle
insisted on looking over her letters that they might not
be a disgrace.   I doubted whether M. le Comte would
have discovered the errors, but when the Marquis praised
some letters that I had written to amuse him from Nancy
and Mezières, she was fired with ambition to write such
clever letters as might bewitch her husband.   Besides,
if she could teach her daughter, the child need not be
banished to a convent.

I began to give her a few lessons in the morning, and
to read to her.   And just then there came to Nid de
Merle, to see me, the good Abbé Bonchamp, the excellent
tutor to whom my dear Philippe always said he owed so
much.   The good man had since had another employment, and on quitting it, could not help gratifying his
desire to come and see the wife and child of his dear
pupil, as indeed I had begged him to do, if ever it were
in his power, when I fulfilled my husband's wishes by
writing his last greeting and final thanks to the good
man.

I remember the dear quaint form riding up on a little hired mule, which he almost concealed with his cassock. Above, his big hat looked so strange that Gaspard, who was wonderfully forward for his age, ran up to me crying: " A droll beast, mamma! it has four legs and a great hat!" while little Armantine fled crying from the monster.

All the servants were, however, coming out eagerly to receive the blessing of the good man, who had made himself much beloved in the household. The Marquis embraced him with tears, and presented him to me, when he fell on his knee, took my hand, pressed it to his lips and bathed it with his tears, and then held Gaspard to his breast with fervent love.

It was necessary to be cheerful before M. de Nidemerle. He had truly loved his nephew, and mourned for him, but the aged do not like a recurrence to sorrows, so the Abbé amused him with the news brought from Saumur, and our party at cards was a complete one that evening.

But the next day, the Abbé, who had loved his pupil like a son, could talk of him to me, and it was a comfort I cannot express to my aching heart to converse with him. Everything had settled into an ordinary course. People fancied me consoled; I had attended to other things, and I could not obtrude my grief on the Marquis or on Cécile; but oh! my sick yearning for my Philippe only grew the more because I might not mention him or hear his name.

However, the Abbé only longed to listen to all I could tell him of the last three years, and in return to tell me much that I should never otherwise have known of the boyhood and youth of my dear one.

I felt as if the good man must never leave us, and I entreated M. de Nidemerle to retain him at once as governor to little Gaspard. The Marquis laughed at securing a tutor for a child not yet three years old; but he allowed that the boy could not be in better hands, and, moreover, he was used to the Abbé, and liked to take his arm and to have him to make up the party at cards, which he played better than the *curé*.

So the Abbé remained as chaplain and as tutor, and, until Gaspard should be old enough to profit by his instructions, Cécile and I entreated him to accept us as pupils. I had begun to feel the need of some hard and engrossing work to take off my thoughts alike from my great sorrow and my pressing anxieties about my English home, so that I wished to return to my Latin studies again, and the Abbé helped me to read *Cicero de Officiis* and likewise some of the writings of St. Gregory the Great. He also read to both of us the Gospels and Mézeray's *History of France,* which I did not know as an adopted Frenchwoman ought to know it, and Cécile knew not at all; nay, the nuns had scarcely taught her any-thing, even about religion, nor the foundations of the faith.

No, I can never explain what we, both of us, owe to the Abbé Bonchamp. You, my eldest grandchild, can just recollect the good old man as he sat in his chair and blessed us ere he passed to his rest and the reward of his labours.

CHAPTER IX.

THE FIREBRAND OF THE BOCAGE.

YES, the life at Nid de Merle was very peaceful. Just as when I look back to my short married life I see how exquisitely happy it was in spite of alarms, anxieties, perplexities, and discomforts, so when I contemplate my three years in Anjou I see that they were full of peace, though the sunshine of my life was over and Cécile's had never come.

We had our children about us, for we took little Maurice d'Aubépine home as soon as possible; we followed the course of devotion and study traced for us by the Abbé ; we attended to the wants of the poor, and taught their children the Catechism ; we worked and lived like sisters, and I thought all that was life to me was over. I forgot that at twenty-two there is much of life yet to come, and that one may go through many a vicissitude of feeling even though one's heart be in a grave.

The old Marquis did not long remain with us. He caught a severe cold in the winter, and had no strength to

rally.   Tryphena would have it that he sank from taking
nothing but *tisanes* made of herbs ; and that if she might
only have given him a good hot sack posset, he would
have recovered; but he shuddered at the thought, and
when a doctor came from Saumur, he bled the poor old
gentleman, faintings came on, and he died the next day.   I
was glad Tryphena's opinion was only expressed in English.

The poor old man had been very kind to me, and had
made me love him better than I should have supposed to
be possible when we crossed from Dover.   The very last
thing he had done was to write to my mother, placing
his hotel at Paris at her disposal in case she and her son
should find it expedient to leave England; and when
his will was opened it proved that he had left me personal guardian and manager of the estates of his heir, my
little Gaspard, now Marquis de Nidemerle, joining no one
with me in the charge but my half-brother the Baron de
Solivet.

I had helped him, read letters to him, and written
them for him, and overlooked his accounts enough for the
work not to be altogether new and strange to me, and I
took it up eagerly.   I had never forgotten the sermon by
the holy Father Vincent, whom the Church has since
acknowledged as a saint, and our excellent Abbé had
heightened the impression that a good work lay prepared
for me ; but he warned me to be prudent, and I am
afraid I was hot-headed and eager.

Much had grieved me in the six months I had spent
in the country, in the state of the peasantry.   I believe
that in the Bocage they are better off than in many parts
of France, but even there they seemed to me much
oppressed and weighed down.   Their huts were wretched
—they had no chimneys, no glass in the windows, no
garden, not even anything comfortable for the old to sit
in ; and when I wanted to give a poor rheumatic old
man a warm cushion, I found it was carefully hidden
away lest M. l'Intendant should suppose the family too
well off.

Those seignorial rights then seemed to me terrible.
The poor people stood in continual fear either of the
intendant of the king or of the Marquis, or of the col-
lector of the dues of the Church.   At harvest time, a
bough was seen sticking in half the sheaves.   In every
ten, one sheaf is marked for the tithe, two for the *seigneur*,
two for the king ; and the officer of each takes the best,
so that only the worst are left for the peasant.

Nay, the only wonder seemed to me that there were
any to be had at all, for our *intendant* thought it his
duty to call off the men from their own fields for the
days due from them whenever he wanted anything to be
done to our land (or his own, or his son's-in-law), without
the slightest regard to the damage their crops suffered
from neglect.

I was sure these things ought not to be.   I thought

infinitely more good might be done by helping the peasants to make the most of what they had, and by preventing them from being robbed in my son's name, than by dealing out gallons of soup and piles of bread at the castle gates to relieve the misery we had brought on them, or by dressing the horrible sores that were caused by dirt and bad food. I told the Abbé, and he said it was a noble inspiration in itself, but that he feared that one lady, and she a foreigner, could not change the customs of centuries, and that innovations were dangerous. I also tried to fire with the same zeal for reformation the Abbess of Bellaise, who was a young and spirited woman, open to conviction; but she was cloistered, and could not go to investigate matters as I did, with the Abbé for my escort, and often with my son. He was enchanted to present any little gift, and it was delightful that the peasants should learn to connect all benefits with Monsieur le Marquis, as they already called the little fellow.

I think they loved me the better when they found that I was the grandchild of the Madame Eustacie who had been hidden in their cottages. I found two or three old people who still remembered her wanderings when she kept the cows and knitted like a peasant girl among them. I was even shown the ruinous chamber where my aunt Thistlewood was born, and the people were enchanted to hear how much the dear old lady had told me of them, and of their ways, and their kindness to her.

I encouraged the people to make their cottages clean and not to be afraid of comforts, promising that our *intendant* at least should not interfere with them. I likewise let him know that I would not have men forced to leave their fields when it would ruin their crops, and that it was better that ours should suffer than theirs. He was obsequious in manner and then disobeyed me, till one day I sent three labourers back again to secure their own hay before they touched ours. And when the harvest was gathered in the Abbé and I went round the fields of the poor, and I pointed out the sheaves that might be marked, and they were not the best.

I taught the girls to knit as they watched their cows, and promised to buy some of their stockings, so that they might obtain *sabots* for themselves with the price. They distrusted me at first, but before long, they began to perceive that I was their friend, and I began to experience a new kind of happiness.

Alas! even this was too sweet to last, or perhaps, as the good Abbé warned me, I was pleasing myself too much with success, and with going my own way. The first murmur of the storm came thus: I had been out all the afternoon with the Abbé, Armantine's *bonne*, and the two elder children, looking at the vineyards, which always interested me much because we have none like them in England. In one, where they were already treading the grapes, the good woman begged that M. le Marquis and

Mademoiselle would for once tread the grapes to bring good luck. They were frantic with joy; we took off their little shoes and silk stockings, rolled them up in thick cloths, and let them get into the trough and dance on the grapes with their little white feet. That wine was always called "the Vintage of le Marquis." We could hardly get them away, they were so joyous, and each carried a great bunch of grapes as a present to the little boy at home and his mother.

We thought we saw a coachman's head and the top of a carriage passing through the lanes, and when we came home I was surprised to find my sister-in-law in tears, thoroughly shaken and agitated.

Mademoiselle de Gringrimeau had been to see her, she said, and had told her the Count was in Paris, but had not sent for her; and I thought that enough to account for her state; but when the children began to tell their eager story, and hold up their grapes to her, she burst again into tears, and cried: " Oh, my dear sister, if you would be warned. It is making a scandal, indeed it is! They call you a plebeian."

I grew hot and angry, and demanded what could be making a scandal, and what business Mademoiselle de Gringrimeau had to meddle with me or my affairs.

" Ah! but she will write to my husband, and he will take me from you, and that would be dreadful. Give it up. Oh, Marguerite, give it up for *my* sake!"

What was I to give up? I demanded. Running about the country, it appeared, like a farmer's wife rather than a lady of quality, and stirring up the poor against their lords. It was well known that all the English were seditious. See what they had done to their king; and here was I, beginning the same work. Had not the Count's *intendant* at Château d'Aubépine thrown in his teeth what Madame de Bellaise did and permitted? He was going to write to Monseigneur, ay, and the king's own *intendant* would hear of it, so I had better take care, and Mademoiselle had come out of pure benevolence to advise Madame la Comtesse to come and take refuge at her husband's own castle before the thunderbolt should fall upon me, and involve her in my ruin.

I laughed. I was sure that I was neither doing nor intending any harm; I thought the whole a mere ebullition of spite on the duenna's part to torment and frighten her emancipated victim, and I treated all as a joke to reassure Cécile, and even laughed at the Abbé for treating the matter more seriously, and saying it was always perilous to go out of a beaten track.

"I thought the beaten track and wide road were the dangerous ones," I said, with more lightness, perhaps, than suited the subject.

"Ah, Madame," he returned gravely, "you have there the truth; but there may be danger in this world in the narrow path."

The most effectual consolation that I could invent for Cécile was that if her husband thought me bad company for her, he could not but fetch her to her proper home with him, as soon as peace was made. Did I really think so? The little thing grew radiant with the hope.

Days went on, we heard nothing, and I was persuaded that the whole had been, as I told Cécile, a mere figment of Mademoiselle de Gringrimeau's.

I had written to beg my mother, with my brother and sister, to come and join us, and I was already beginning to arrange a suite of rooms for them, my heart bounding as it only can do at the thought of meeting those nearest and dearest of one's own blood.

I remember that I was busy giving orders that the linen should be aired, and overlooking the store of sheets, when Gaspard and Armantine from the window called out: " Horses, horses, mamma! fine cavaliers!"

I rushed to the window and recognised the Solivet colours. No doubt the baron had come to announce the arrival of my mother and the rest, and I hastened down to meet him at the door, full of delight, with my son holding my hand.

My first exclamation after the greeting was to ask where they were, and how soon they would arrive, and I was terribly disappointed when I found that he had come alone, and that my mother, with Eustace and Annora, were at the Hôtel de Nidemerle, at Paris, without any intention of leaving it. He himself had come down on business, as indeed was only natural since he was joined with me in the guardianship of my little Marquis, and he would likewise be in time to enjoy the chase over the estates.

He said no more of his purpose then, so I was not alarmed; and he seemed much struck with the growth and improvement of Gaspard. I had much to hear of the three who were left to me of my own family. M. de Solivet had never seen them before, and could hardly remember his mother, so he could not compare them with what they were before their troubles; but I gathered that my mother was well in health, and little the worse for all her troubles, and that my little Nan was as tall as myself, a true White Ribaumont, with an exquisite complexion, who would be all the rage if she were not so extremely English, more English even than I had been when I had arrived.

"And my brother, my Eustace. Oh, why did he not come with you?" I asked.

And M. de Solivet gravely answered that our brother was detained by a suit with the Poligny family respecting the estate of Ribaumont, and, besides, that the rapidity of the journey would not have agreed with his state of health. I only then fully understood the matter, for our letters had been few, and had to be carefully written and made short; and though I knew that, at the battle of

Naseby, Eustace had been wounded and made prisoner, he
had written to me that his hurt was not severe, and that
he had been kindly treated, through the intervention of
our cousin Harry Merrycourt, who, to our great regret,
was among the rebels, but who had become surety for
Eustace and procured his release.

I now heard that my brother had been kept with the
other prisoners in a miserable damp barn, letting in the
weather on all sides, and with no bedding or other comforts, so that when Harry Merrycourt sought him out,
he had taken a violent chill, and had nearly died, not
from the wound, but from pleurisy. He had never
entirely recovered, though my mother thought him much
stronger and better since he had been in France, out of
sight of all that was so sad and grievous to a loyal
cavalier in England.

"They must come to me," I cried. "He will soon
be well in this beautiful air; I will feed him with goat's
milk and whey, and Tryphena shall nurse him well."

M. de Solivet made no answer to this, but told me
how delighted the Queen of England had been to welcome
my mother, whom she had at once appointed as one of
her ladies of the bedchamber; and then we spoke of
King Charles, who was at Hampton Court, trying to
make terms with the Parliament, and my brother spoke
with regret and alarm of the like spirit of resistance in
our own Parliament of Paris, backed by the mob.   I

remember it was on that evening that I first heard the
name Frondeurs, or Slingers, applied to the speechifiers
on either side who started forward, made their hit, and
retreated, like the little street boys with their slings.   I
was to hear a great deal more of that name.

It was not till after supper that I heard the cause of
M. de Solivet's visit. Cécile, who always retired early,
went away sooner than usual to leave us together, so did
the Abbé, and then the baron turned to me and said :
" Sister, how soon can you be prepared to come with me
to Paris ? "

I was astounded, thinking at first that Eustace's
illness must be more serious than he had led me to suppose, but he smiled and said *nòtre frère de Volvent,* which
was the nearest he could get to Walwyn, had nothing to
do with it; it was by express command of the Queen-
Regent, and that I might thank my mother and the
Queen of England that it was no worse. " This is better
than a *lettre de cachet,*" he added, producing a magnificent-
looking envelope with a huge seal of the royal French
arms, that made me laugh rather nervously to brave my
dismay, and asked what he called *that.* He responded
gravely that it was no laughing matter, and I opened
it.   It was an official order that Gaspard Philippe
Béranger de Bellaise, Marquis de Nidemerle, should
be brought to the Louvre to be presented to the
King.

"Well," I said, "I must go to Paris. Ought I to have brought my boy before? I did not know that he ought to pay his homage till he was older. Was it really such a breach of respect?"

"You are a child yourself, my sister," he said, much injuring my dignity. "What have you not been doing here?"

Then it came on me. The *intendant* of the King had actually written complaints of me to the Government. I was sowing disaffection among the peasants by the favours I granted my own, teaching them to dispute seignorial rights, and preparing them for rebellion like that which raged in England, and bringing up my son in the same sentiments. Nay, I was called the Firebrand of the Bocage! If these had been the days of the great Cardinal de Richelieu, my brother assured me, I should probably have been by this time in the Bastille, and my son would have been taken from me for ever!

However, my half-brother heard of it in time, and my mother had flown to Queen Henrietta, who took her to the Queen-Regent, and together they had made such representations of my youth, folly, and inexperience, that the Queen-Mother, who had a fellow-feeling for a young widow and her son, had at last consented to do nothing worse than summon me and my child to Paris, where my mother and her Queen answered for me that I should live quietly, and give no more umbrage to the authorities; and my brother De Solivet had been sent off to fetch me!

I am afraid I was much more angry than grateful,
and I said such hot things about tyranny, cruelty, and
oppression, that Solivet looked about in alarm, lest walls
should have ears, and told me he feared he had done
wrong in answering for me. He was really a good man,
but he could not in the least understand why I should
weep hot tears for my poor people whom I was just
hoping to benefit. He could not enter into feeling for
Jacques Bonhomme so much as for his horse or his dog;
and I might have argued for years without making him see
anything but childish folly in my wishing for any mode
of relief better than doles of soup, dressing of wounds,
and dowries for maidens.

However, there was no choice; I was helpless, and
resistance would have done my people no good, but
rather harm, and would only have led to my son being
separated from me. Indeed, I cherished a hope that
when the good Queen Anne heard the facts she might
understand better than my half-brother did, and that
I might become an example and public benefactor. My
brother must have smiled at me in secret, but he did
not contradict me.

My poor mother and the rest would not have been
flattered by my reluctance to come to Paris; but in truth
the thought of them was my drop of comfort, and if
Eustace could not come to me I must have gone to him.
And Cécile—what was to become of Cécile?

To come with me of course. Here at least Solivet agreed with me, for he had as great a horror of Mademoiselle de Gringrimeau as I had, and knew, moreover, that she wrote spiteful letters to the Count d'Aubépine about his poor little wife, which happily were treated with the young gentleman's usual *insouciance.* Solivet was of my opinion that the old demoiselle had instigated this attack. He thought so all the more when he heard that she was actually condescending to wed the *intendant* of Château d'Aubépine. But he said he had no doubt that my proceedings would have been stopped sooner or later, and that it was well that it should be done before I committed myself unpardonably.

Madame d'Aubépine had been placed in my charge by her husband, so that I was justified in taking her with me. Her husband had spent the last winter at Paris, but was now with the army in the Low Countries, and the compliments Solivet paid me on my dear friend's improvement in appearance and manner inspired us with strong hopes that she might now attract her husband; for though still small, pale, and timid, she was very unlike the frightened sickly child he had left.

I believe she was the one truly happy person when we left the Château de Nid de Merle. She was all radiant with hope and joy, and my brother could not but confess she was almost beautiful, and a creature whom any man with a heart must love.

CHAPTER X.

OLD THREADS TAKEN UP.

I THINK M. de Solivet realised a little better what the sacrifice was to me, or rather how cruel the parting was to my poor people, when we set forth on our journey. We had tried to keep the time of our departure a secret, but it had not been possible to do so, and the whole court was filled with people weeping and crying out to their young lord and their good lady, as they called me, not to abandon them, kissing our dresses as we walked along, and crowding so that we could hardly pass.

Indeed, a lame man, whom I had taught to make mats, threw himself before the horses of our carriage, crying out that we might as well drive over him and kill him at once; and an old woman stood up almost like a witch or prophetess, crying out: " Ah! that is the way with you all. You are like all the rest! You gave us hope once, and now you are gone to your pleasures which you squeeze out of our hearts' blood."

" Ah, good mother," I said; " believe me, it is not

by my own will that I leave you; I will never forget you."

"I trust," muttered Solivet, "that no one is here to report all this to that *Intendant du Roi*," and he hurried me into the carriage; but there were tears running down his cheeks, and I believe he emptied his purse among them, though not without being told by some of the poor warm-hearted creatures that no money could repay them for the loss of Madame la Vicomtesse.

: "I did not know how sweet it is to be beloved," he said to me. "It is almost enough to tempt one to play the *rôle de bon seigneur*."

"Ah! brother, if you would. You are no foreigner, you are wiser and would not make yourself suspected like me."

He only laughed and shrugged his shoulders; but he was as good to our poor as it is possible to be as we live here in France, where we are often absolutely compelled to live at court, and our expenses there force us to press heavily on our already hard-driven peasants. I sometimes wonder whether a better time will come, when our good Duke of Burgundy tries to carry out the maxims of Monseigneur the Archbishop of Cambray; but I shall not live to see that day.[1]

In due time we arrived in Paris. It was pouring

---

[1] No wonder Madame de Bellaise's descendants durst not publish these writings while the *ancien régime* continued!

with rain, so no one came to meet us, though I looked
out at every turn, feeling that Eustace must indeed be
unwell, or no weather would have kept him from flying
to meet his Meg.   Or had he in these six long years
ceased to care for me, and should I find him a politician
and a soldier, with his heart given to somebody else and
no room for me?

My heart beat so fast that I could hardly attend to
the cries of wonder and questions of the two children, and
indeed of Cécile, to whom everything was as new and
wonderful as to them, though in the wet, with our
windows splashed all over, the first view of Paris was not
too promising.   However, at last we drove beneath our
own *porte cochère*, and upon the steps there were all the
servants.   And Eustace, my own dear brother, was at the
coach-door to meet us and hand me out.

I passed from his arms to those of my mother, and
then to my sister's.   Whatever might come and go, I
could not but feel that there was an indefinable bliss and
bien-être in their very presence!   It was home—coming
home—more true content and rest than I had felt since
that fatal day at Nancy.

My mother was enchanted with her grandson, and
knew how to welcome Madame d'Aubépine as one of
the family, since she was of course to reside with us.
The Abbé also was most welcome to my mother.

How we all looked at one another, to find the old

beings we had loved, and to learn the new ones we had become! My mother was of course the least altered; indeed, to my surprise, she was more *embonpoint* than before, instead of having the haggard worn air that I had expected, and though she wept at first, she was soon again smiling.

Eustace, Baron Walwyn and Ribaumont, as he now unfortunately had become, sat by me. He was much taller than when we had parted, for he had not then reached his full height, and he looked the taller from being very thin. His moustache and pointed beard had likewise changed him, but there was clear bright colour on his cheek, and his dear brown eyes shone upon me with their old sweetness; so that it was not till we had been together some little time that I found that the gay merry lad whom I had left had become not only a man, but a very grave and thoughtful man.

Annora was a fine creature, well grown, and with the clearest, freshest complexion, of the most perfect health, yet so pure and delicate, that one looked at her like a beautiful flower; but it somehow struck me that she had a discontented and almost defiant expression. She seemed to look at me with a sort of distrust, and to be with difficulty polite to Madame d'Aubépine, while she was almost rude to the Abbé. She scarcely uttered a word of French, and made a little cry and gesture of disgust, when Gaspard replied to her in his native tongue, poor child.

She was the chief disappointment to me. I had expected to find, not indeed my little playfellow, but my own loving sister Nan ; and this young lady was like a stranger. I thought, too, my mother would have been less lively, but she seemed to me to have forgotten everything in the satisfaction of being at Paris. At first I feared she was looking at me with displeasure, but presently I observed that she had discarded her widow's veil, and looked annoyed that I still wore mine. Otherwise she was agreeably surprised in me, and turned to M. de Solivet, saying:

" Yes, my son, you are right, she is *belle, assez belle ;* and when she is dressed and has no more that provincial air, she will do very well."

It was Eustace, my brother, who gave me unmixed delight that evening, unmixed save for his look of delicate health, for that he should be graver was only suitable to my feelings, and we knew that we were in perfect sympathy with one another whenever our eyes met, as of old, while we had hardly exchanged a word. And then, how gracious and gentle he was with poor little Madame d'Aubépine, who looked up to him like a little violet at the foot of a poplar tree !

Supper passed in inquiries after kinsfolk and old friends. Alas! of how many the answer was—slain, missing since such a battle. In prison, ruined, and brought to poverty, seemed to be the best I could hear of any one I inquired after. That Walwyn was not yet utterly lost seemed to be owing to Harry Merry-court.

"He on the wrong side !" I exclaimed.

"He looks on the question as a lawyer," said my brother ; "holding the duty of the nation to be rather to the law than to the sovereign."

"Base! Unworthy of a gentleman!" cried my mother. "Who would believe him the kinsman of the gallant Duc de Méricour ?"

"He would be ashamed to count kindred with that effeminate *petit maître !*" cried Annora.

"I think," said Eustace, "that the wrong and persecution that his Huguenot grandfather suffered at the hands of his French family have had much power in inspiring him with that which he declares is as much loyalty as what I call by that honoured name."

"You can speak of him with patience !" cried my mother.

"In common gratitude he is bound to do so," said Annora.

For not only had Colonel Merrycourt preserved our brother's life after Naseby, but he had found a plea of service to the King which availed at the trial that followed at Westminster. Harry had managed to secure part of the estate, as he had likewise done for our other kindred the Thistlewoods, by getting appointed their

guardian when their father was killed at Chalgrove. But
soldiers had been quartered on both families; there had
been a skirmish at Walwyn with Sir Ralph Hopton, much
damage had been done to the house and grounds, and
there was no means of repairing it; all the plate had
been melted up, there was nothing to show for it but
a little oval token, with the King's head on one side,
and the Queen's on the other; and as to the chaplet of
pearls—

There was a moment's silence as I inquired for them.
Annora said:

"Gone, of course; more hatefully than all the rest."

My brother added, with a smile that evidently cost
him an effort:

"You are the only pearl of Ribaumont left, Meg,
except this one," showing me his ring of thin silver with
one pearl set in it; "I kept back this one in memory of
my grandmother. So Nan will have to go to her first
ball without them."

And had little Nan never been to a ball? No; she
had never danced except that Christmas when a troop of
cavaliers had been quartered at Walwyn—a merry young
captain and his lieutenant, who had sent for the fiddles,
and made them have a dance in the hall, Berenger, and
Nan, and all. And not a week· after, the young captain,
ay, and our dear Berry, were lying in their blood at Alresford. Had Nan's heart been left there? I wondered,

when I saw how little she brightened at the mention of
the Court ball where she was to appear next week, and
to which it seemed my mother trusted that I should be
invited in token of my being forgiven.

I tried to say that I had never meant to return to the
world, and that I still kept to my mourning; but my
mother said with authority that I had better be grateful
for any token of favour that was vouchsafed to me.   She
took me into her own apartment after supper, and talked
to me very seriously; telling me that I must be
very careful, for that I had been so imprudent, that I
should certainly have been deprived of the custody of my
son, if not imprisoned, unless my good godmother, Queen
Henrietta, and herself had made themselves responsible
for me.

I told my mother that I had done nothing, absolutely
nothing, but attend to the wants of my son's people, just
as I had been used to see my grandmother, and my aunt
Thistlewood, or any English lady, do at home.

" And to what has that brought England ?" cried my
mother.   " No, child, those creatures have no gratitude
nor proper feeling.   There is nothing to do but to keep
them down.   See how they are hampering and impeding
the Queen and the Cardinal here, refusing the registry of
the taxes forsooth, as if it were not honour enough to
maintain the King's wars and the splendour of his Court,
and enable the nobility to shine !"

"Surely it is our duty to do something for them in return," I said; but I was silenced with assurances that if I wished to preserve the wardship of my child, I must conform in everything; nay, that my own liberty was in danger.

Solivet had hinted as much, and the protection of my child was a powerful engine; but—shall I confess it?— it galled and chafed me terribly to feel myself taken once more into leading-strings. I, who had for three years governed my house as a happy honoured wife, and for three more had been a *châtelaine*, complimented by the old uncle, and after his death, the sole ruler of my son's domain; I was not at all inclined to return into tutelage, and I could not look on my mother after these six years, as quite the same conclusive authority as I thought her when I left her. The spirit of self-assertion and self-justification was strong within me, and though I hope I did not reply with ingratitude or disrespect, I would make no absolute promise till I had heard what my brother Walwyn said of my position in its secular aspect, and the Abbé Bonchamps in its religious point of view. So I bade my mother good-night, and went to see how Cécile fared in her new quarters, which, to her grief, were in a wing separated from mine by a long corridor.

My mother had arranged everything, ruling naturally as if she were the mistress of the house. Thus she installed me in the great room where I had seen the old

Marquise, though I would rather she had retained it, and given me that which I had occupied when I was there with my husband. However, I made no objection, for I felt so much vexed that I was extremely afraid of saying something to show that I thought she ought to remember that this was my house, and that she was my guest. I would not for the world have uttered anything so ungenerous and unfilial; and all I could do that night was to pray that she might not drive me to lose my self-command, and that I might both do right and keep my child.

I was too restless and unhappy to sleep much, for I knew my feelings were wrong, and yet I was sure I was in the right in my wish to do good to the poor ; and the sense of being bridled, and put into leading-strings, poisoned the pleasure I had at first felt in my return to my own family. I cannot describe the weary tumult of thought and doubt that tossed me, till, after a brief sleep, I heard the church-bells. I rose and dressed for early mass, taking my boy, who always awoke betimes, leaving the house quietly, and only calling my trusty lackey Nicolas to take me to the nearest Church, which was not many steps off. I do not think I found peace there : there was too much *self* in me to reach that as yet ; but at any rate I found the resolution to try to bend my will in what might be indifferent, and to own it to be wholesome for me to learn submission once more.

As I was about to enter our court, I heard a little

cough, and looking round I saw a gentleman and lady coming towards the house. They were my brother and sister, who had been to the daily prayers at the house of Sir Richard Browne, the English ambassador. I was struck at my first glance with the lightsome free look of Annora's face, but it clouded and grew constrained in an instant when I spoke to her.

They said my mother would not be awake nor admit us for an hour or two, and in the meantime Eustace was ready to come to my apartments, for indeed we had hardly seen one another. Annora anxiously reminded him that he must take his chocolate, and orders were given that this should be served in my cabinet for us both.

There is no describing what that interview was to us. We, who had been one throughout our childhood, but had been parted all through the change to man and woman, now found ourselves united again, understanding one another as no other being could do, and almost without words, entering into full sympathy with one another. Yes, without words, for I was as certain as if he had told me that Eustace had undergone some sorrow deeper than even loss of health, home, and country. I felt it in the chastened and sobered tone in which he talked to me of my cares, as if he likewise had crossed the stream of tears that divides us from the sunshine of our lives.

He did not think what I had attempted in Anjou foolish and chimerical—he could look at the matter with

the eyes of an English lord of the manor, accustomed not
to view the peasant as a sponge to be squeezed for the
benefit of the master, but to regard the landlord as account-
able for the welfare, bodily and spiritual, of his people.
He thought I had done right, though it might be ignorantly
and imprudently in the present state of things ; but his
heart had likewise burned within him at the oppression of
the peasantry, and, loyal cavalier as he was, he declared
that he should have doubted on which side to draw
his sword had things been thus in England. He had
striven to make my mother and Queen Henrietta understand the meaning of what I had been doing, and he
said the complaints sent up had evidently been much
exaggerated, and envenomed by spite and distrust of me
as a foreigner. He could well enter into my grief at the
desertion of my poor people, for how was it with those at
Walwyn, deprived of the family to whom they had been
used to look, with many widows and orphans made by
the war, and the Church invaded by a loud-voiced empty-
headed fanatic, who had swept away all that had been
carefully preserved and honoured ! Should he ever see
the old home more ?

However, he took thought for my predicament. I
had no choice, he said, but to give way. To resist would
only make me be treated as a suspected person, and be
relegated to a convent, out of reach of influencing my son,
whom I might bring up to be a real power for good.

Then my dear brother smiled his sweetest smile, the sweeter for the sadness that had come into it, and kissed my fingers chivalrously, as he said that after all he could not but be grateful to the edict that had brought back to him the greatest delight that was left to him. "Ah," I said, "if it had only been in Anjou!"

"If it had only been in Dorset, let us say at once," he answered.

Then came the other question whether I might not stay at home with the children, and give myself to devotion and good works, instead of throwing off my mourning and following my mother to all the gaieties of the court.

"My poor mother!" said Eustace. "You would not wish to make your example a standing condemnation of ⋅ her?"

"I cannot understand how she᾽ can find pleasure in these things," I cried.

"There is much in her that we find it hard to understand," Eustace said; "but you must remember that this is her own country, and that though she gave it up for my father's sake, England has always been a land of exile to her, and we cannot wonder at her being glad to return to the society of her old friends."

"She has Annora to be with her. Is not that enough?"

"Ah, Meg, I trusted to you to soothe poor Annora and make her more conformable."

"She seems to have no intention of putting herself under my influence," I said, rather hurt.

"She soon will, when she finds out your English heart," said Eustace. "The poor child is a most unwilling exile, and is acting like our old friends the urchins, opposing the prickles to all. But if my mother has Annora to watch over, you also have a charge. A boy of this little man's rank," he said, stroking the glossy curls of Gaspard, who was leaning on my lap, staring up in wonder at the unknown tongue spoken by his uncle, "and so near the age of the king, will certainly be summoned to attend at court, and if you shut yourself up, you will be unable to follow him and guide him by your counsel."

That was the chief of what my dear brother said to me on that morning. I wrote it down at the moment because, though I trusted his wisdom and goodness with all my heart, I thought his being a Protestant might bias his views in some degree, and I wanted to know whether the Abbé thought me bound by my plans of devotion, which happily had not been vows.

And he fully thought my brother in the right, and that it was my duty to remain in the world, so long as my son needed me there; while, as to any galling from coming under authority again, that was probably exactly what my character wanted, and it would lessen the danger of dissipation. Perhaps I might have been in more real danger in queening it at Nid de Merle than in submitting at Paris.

CHAPTER XI.

THE TWO QUEENS.

AFTER all, I was put to shame by finding that I had
done my poor mother an injustice in supposing that she
intended to assume the government of the house, for no
sooner was I admitted to her room than she gave me up
the keys, and indeed I believe she was not sorry to resign
them, for she had not loved housewifery in her prosperous days, and there had been a hard struggle with
absolute poverty during the last years in England.

She was delighted likewise that I was quite ready to
accompany her to thank Queen Henrietta for her inter-
cession, and to take her advice for the future, nor did she
object for that day to my mourning costume, as I was to
appear in the character of a suppliant. When I caught
Annora's almost contemptuous eye, I was ready to have
gone in diamonds and feathers.

However, forth we set, attended by both my brothers.
Lord Walwyn indeed held some appointment at the little
court, and in due time we were ushered into the room

where Queen Henrietta was seated with a pretty little girl playing at her feet with a dog, and a youth of about seventeen leaning over the elbow of her couch telling her something with great animation, while a few ladies were at work, with gentlemen scattered among them. How sociable and friendly it looked, and how strangely yet pleasantly the English tones fell on my ear! And I was received most kindly too. " Madame has brought her— our little—nay, our great conspirator, the Firebrand of the Bocage. Come, little Firebrand," exclaimed the Queen, and as I knelt to kiss her hand she threw her arms round me in an affectionate embrace, and the Prince of Wales claimed me as an old acquaintance, saluted me, and laughed, as he welcomed me to their court of waifs and strays, cast up one by one by the tide.

His little sister, brought by the faithful Lady Morton in the disguise of a beggar boy, had been the last thus to arrive. A very lovely child she was, and Prince Charles made every one laugh by taking her on his knee and calling her Piers the beggar boy, when she pointed to her white frock, called herself " Pincess, pincess, not beggar boy," and when he persisted, went into a little rage and pulled his black curls.

My poor Queen, whom I had left in the pride and mature bloom of beauty, was sadly changed; she looked thin and worn, and was altogether the brown old French-woman ; but she was still as lively and vivacious, and full of arch kindness as ever, a true daughter of the *Grand Monarque*, whose spirits no disasters could break. When the little one became too noisy, she playfully ordered off both the children, as she called them, and bade me sit down on the footstool before her couch, and tell her what I had been doing to put *intendants*, cardinals, and Queens themselves into commotion. The little Lady Henrietta was carried off by one of the attendants, but the Prince would not go; he resumed his former position, saying that he was quite sure that Madame de Bellaise was in need of an English counsel to plead her cause. He had grown up from a mischievous imp of a boy to a graceful elegant-looking youth. His figure, air, and address were charming, I never saw them equalled; but his face was as ugly as ever, though with a droll ugliness that was more winning than most men's beauty, lighted up as it was by the most brilliant of black eyes and the most engaging of smiles. You remember that I am speaking of him as he was when he had lately arrived from Jersey, before his expedition to Scotland. He became a very different person after his return, but he was now a simple-hearted, innocent lad, and I met him again as an old friend and playfellow, whose sympathy was a great satisfaction in the story I had to tell, though it was given in a half-mocking way. My mother began by saying:

"The poor child, it is as I told your Majesty; she has only been a little too charitable."

" Permit me, Madame," I said, " I did not give half so much as most charitable ladies."

Then the explanation came, and the Queen shook her head and told me such things would not do here, that my inexperience might be pardonable, but that the only way to treat such creatures was to feed them and clothe them for the sake of our own souls.

Here the Prince made his eyes first flash and then wink at me.

" But as to teaching them or elevating them, my dear, it is as bad for them as for ourselves. You must renounce all such chimeras, and if you have a passion for charity there is good Father Vincent to teach you safe methods."

I brightened up when I heard of Father Vincent, and my mother engaged for me that I should do all that was right, and appealed to my brother De Solivet to assure the Queen that there had been much malignant exaggeration about the presumption of my measures and the discontent of other people's peasants.

Queen Henrietta was quite satisfied, and declared that she would at once conduct me to her sister-in-law, the Queen-Regent, at the Tuileries, since she had of course the "petites entrées," take her by storm as it were, and it was exactly the right hour when the Queen would be resting after holding council.

She called for a looking-glass, and made one of her

women touch up her dress and bring her a fan, asking
whether I had ever been presented. No, my first stay
at Paris had been too short; besides, my rank did not
make it needful, as my husband was only Viscount by
favour of his uncle, who let him hold the estate.

"Then," said the Prince, "you little know what court
is!"

"Can you make a curtsey?" asked the Queen anxiously.

I repeated the one I had lately made to her Majesty,
and they all cried out :

"Oh, oh! that was all very well at home."

"Or here before I married," added Queen Henrietta.
"Since Spanish etiquette has come in, we have all been
on our good behaviour."

"Having come from a barbarous isle," added the
Prince.

The Queen therewith made the reverence which you
all know, my grand-daughters, but which seemed to me
unnatural, and the Prince's face twinkled at the incredulity he saw in mine; but at that moment a private door
was opening to give admission to a figure, not in itself
very tall, but looking twice its height from its upright,
haughty bearing. There was the Bourbon face fully
marked, with a good deal of fair hair in curls round it,
and a wonderful air of complete self-complacency.

This was *la grande Mademoiselle*, daughter of Gaston,
Duke of Orleans, and heiress through her mother of the

great old Montpensier family, who lived at the Palais
Royal with her father, but was often at the Louvre. She
stood aghast, as well she might, thinking how little
dignity her aunt, the Queen of England, had to be acting
as mistress of deportment to a little homely widow. The
Prince turned at once.

" There is my cousin," said he, " standing amazed to
see how we have caught a barbarous islander of our own,
and are trying to train her to civilisation. Here—let
her represent the Queen-Regent. Now, Meg—Madame
de Bellaise, I mean—imitate me while my mother pre-
sents me," he ran on in English, making such a grotesque
reverence that nobody except Mademoiselle could help
laughing, and his mother made a feint of laying her fan
about his ears, while she pronounced him a madcap and
begged her niece to excuse him.

" For profaning the outskirts of the majesty of the
Most Christian King," muttered the Prince, while his
mother explained the matter to her niece, adding that
her son could not help availing himself of the opportunity of paying her his homage.

Mademoiselle was pacified, and was graciously pleased
to permit me to be presented to her, also to criticise the
curtsey which I had now to perform, my good Queen
being so kind in training me that I almost lost the sense
of the incongruity of such a lesson at my age and in my
weeds. In fact, with my mother and my godmother

commanding me, and Eustace and the Prince of Wales looking on, it was like a return to one's childhood. At last I satisfied my royal instructress, and as she agreed with my mother that my mourning befitted the occasion, off we set *en grande tenue* to cross the court to the Tuileries in a little procession, the Queen, attended by my mother and Lady Morton as her ladies, and by Lord Jermyn and Eustace as her gentlemen-in-waiting.

Mademoiselle also came, out of a sort of good-natured curiosity, but the Prince of Wales shook his head.

"I have no mind to show Madame the value of a *tabouret*," he said. "Believe me, Meg, I may sit on such an eminence in the august presence of my mother and my regent aunt, but if my small cousin, the Most Christian King, should enter, I must be dethroned, and a succession of bows must ensue before we can either of us be seated. I always fear that I shall some day break out with the speech of King Lear's fool: 'Cry you mercy, I took you for a joint stool.'"

This passed while I, who came in the rear of the procession, was waiting to move on, and I believe Queen Henrietta was descanting to her niece on the blessing that her son's high spirits never failed him through all their misfortunes.

However, in due time we reached the apartments of the Queen-Regent, the way lined with guards, servants,

and splendid gentlemen, who all either presented arms
or bowed as our English Queen passed along, with an
easy, frank majesty about her that bespoke her a
daughter of the place, and at home there. But what
gave me the most courage was that as the door of her
bedroom was opened to admit Queen Henrietta, Mademoiselle, my mother, and myself, I saw a black cassock,
and a face I knew again as that of the Holy Father,
Vincent de Paul, who had so much impressed me, and
had first given me comfort.

It was a magnificent room, and more magnificent
bed, and sitting up among her lace and cambric pillows
and coverlets was Queen Anne of Austria, in a rich
white lace cap and bedgown that set off her smooth, fair,
plump beauty, and exquisite hands and arms. Ladies
stood round the bed. I did not then see who any of
them were, for this was the crisis of my fate, and my
heart beat and my eyes swam with anxiety. Queen
Henrietta made her low reverence, as of course we did,
and some words of sisterly greeting ensued, after which
the English queen said :

" My sister, I have made you this early visit to bring
you my little suppliant. Allow me to present to your
Majesty, Madame la Vicomtesse de Bellaise, who is
sincerely sorry to have offended you."

(That was true ; I was sincerely sorry that what I
had done could offend.)

My kind godmother went on to say that I had
offended only out of ignorance of the rights of *seigneurs*,
and from my charitable impulses, of which she knew
that her Majesty would approve, glancing significantly
towards Father Vincent as she did so.   She was sure,
she added, that Her Majesty's tenderness of heart must
sympathise with a young widow, whose husband had
fallen in the service of the King, and who had an only
son to bring up.   I felt the Regent's beautiful blue
eyes scanning me, but it was not unkindly, though she
said :

"How is this, Madame ?   I hear that you have
taught the peasants to complain of the seignorial rights,
and to expect to have the *corvée* and all other dues
remitted."

I made answer that in truth all I had done was to
remit those claims here and there which had seemed to
me to press hard upon the tenants of our own estate ;
and I think the Regent was moved by a look from Father
Vincent to demand an example, so I mentioned that I
would not have the poor forced to carry our crops on the
only fine day in a wet season.

"Ah, bah !" said Queen Anne; "that was an over-
refinement, Madame.   It does not hurt those creatures to
get wet."

She really had not the least notion that a wetting
ruined their crops ; and when I would have answered,

my godmother and mother made me a sign to hold my
tongue, while Queen Henrietta spoke :

"Your Majesty sees how it is ; my godchild has the
enthusiasm of charity, and you, my sister, with your
surroundings, will not blame her if she has carried it a
little into excess."

"Your Majesty will pardon me for asking if there
can be excess ?" said Father Vincent.   "I think I recognise this lady.   Did I not meet Madame at the little
village of St. Félix ?"

"Oh yes, my father," I replied.   "I have ever since
blessed the day, when you comforted me and gave me
the key of life."

"There, father," said the Regent, "it is your doing ;
it is you that have made her a firebrand.   You must
henceforth take the responsibility."

"I ask no better of your Majesty," said the holy man.

"Ah! your Majesty, I can ask no better," I said
fervently ; and I knelt to kiss the beautiful hand which
Anne of Austria extended to me in token of pardon.

"It is understood, then," said she, in a gracious though
languid way, as if weary of the subject, "that your Majesty
undertakes that Madame becomes more prudent in the
future, and puts her benevolence under the rule of our
good father, who will never let her go beyond what is
wise in the bounds of a young woman's discretion."

It might be hard to believe that I had been

indiscreet, but the grand stately self-possession of
that Spanish lady, and the evident gratification of my
mother and Queen Henrietta, quite overpowered me into
feeling like a criminal received to mercy, and I returned
thanks with all the genuine humility they could desire ;
after which the regent overpowered my mother with
wonder at her graciousness by inquiring for my son,
asking how old he was, and appointing a day for him to
kiss the King's hand in the Tuileries gardens.

By this time her breakfast was being brought in (it
was about one o'clock), and Queen Henrietta carried us
off without waiting for the ceremony of the breakfast, or
of the toilet, which began with the little King presenting
his mother with her chemise, with a tender kiss. Mademoiselle remained, and so did Father Vincent, whom the
regent was wont to consult at her breakfast, both on
matters of charity and of Church patronage.

My mother was delighted that I had come off so well;
she only regretted my being put under Father Vincent,
who would, she feared, render me too devout.

The next afternoon, which was Sunday, we went, all
except my brother and sister, who had what my mother
called Puritan notions as to Sunday, to see royalty walk
in the Tuileries gardens. The Queen was there, slowly
pacing along with one of her sons on each side, and
beautiful boys they were, in their rich dresses of blue
velvet and white satin, with rich lace garnishings, their

long fair hair on their shoulders, and their plumed hats less often on their heads than in their hands, as they gracefully acknowledged the homage that met them at each step. Perhaps I thought my Gaspard quite as beautiful, but every widow's only son is *the* king of her heart; and we had so trained the boy that he did his part to perfection, kneeling and kissing the hand which King Louis extended to him. Yet it had—to me who was fresh to such scenes—something of the air of a little comedy, to see such gestures of respect between the two children so splendidly dressed, and neither of them yet nine years old.

The little King did his part well, presented M. le Marquis de Nidemerle to his brother the Duke of Anjou, asked graciously whether he could ride and what games he loved best, and expressed a courteous desire that they might often meet.

My sister-in-law was also presented to the Queen, who filled her with ecstasy by making her some compliment on the services of M. le Comte d'Aubépine, and thus began our career at court. We were in favour, and my mother breathed freely.

CHAPTER XII.

CAVALIERS IN EXILE.

MY safety and freedom being thus secure, I was asked, as mistress of the house, whether I would continue the custom my mother had begun of receiving on a Monday, chiefly for the sake of our exiled countryfolk at Paris.

It had been left in doubt, till my fate and my wishes should be known, whether the reunion should take place on the Monday or not; but all lived so simply and within so short a distance that it was very easy to make it known that Lady Walwyn and Madame de Bellaise would receive as usual.

The rule in ordinary French society was then as now, to offer only *eau-sucrée*, sherbets, and light cakes as refreshments, but my mother told me with some disgust that it was necessary to have something more substantial on the buffet for these great Englishmen.

" Yes," said Annora, " I do believe it is often the only meal worth the name that they get in a week, unless my brother invites them to supper."

On learning this Tryphena and I resolved that though pies were the most substantial dish at present prepared, we would do our best another time to set before them such a round of salt beef as would rejoice their appetites; and oh! the trouble we had in accomplishing it.

Meantime I submitted to be dressed as my mother wished, much indeed as I am now, except that my hair was put into little curls, and I had no cap. The Queen-Regent wore none, so why should I? Moreover, my mother said that it would not be good taste to put on any jewels among the English.

Alas! I could see why, as the *salon* filled with gentlemen and ladies, far fewer of the last than the first, for some wives had been left at home with their children to keep possession of the estates, and send what supplies they could to their lords in exile. Some, like brave Lady Fanshawe, travelled backwards and forwards again and again on their husbands' affairs; and some who were at Paris could not afford a servant nor leave their little children, and others had no dress fit to appear in. And yet some of the dresses were shabby enough—frayed satin or faded stained brocade, the singes and the creases telling of hard service and rough usage. The gentlemen were not much better: some had their velvet coats worn wofully at the elbows, and the lace of their collars darned; indeed those were the best off, for there were

some who had no ladies to take care of them, whose fine
Flanders lace was in terrible holes.

Some gallants indeed there were to ruffle it as sprucely
as ever, and there were a few who had taken service as
musketeers or archers of the guard ; but these were at that
time few, for the King was still living, and they did not
despair of an accommodation which would soon bring
them home again. As my mother had predicted, the
gentlemen with the ragged lace tried in vain to affect
indifference to the good things on the buffet, till they had
done their *devoir* by me as their hostess. Eustace and
Nan were on the watch and soon were caring for them,
and heaping their plates with food, and then it was that
my sister's face began to light up, and I knew her for
herself again, while there was a general sound of full gruff
English voices all round, harsh and cracking my mother
called it, but Nan said it was perfect music to her, and
I think she began to forgive me when she found that to
me likewise it had a sound of home.

But my mother was greatly gratified that evening,
for there appeared in our *salon* the dark bright face of
the Prince of Wales, closely followed by a tall handsome man in the prime of life, whom I had never seen
before.

"Do not derange yourself," said Prince Charles,
bending his black head, bowing right and left, and signing
with his hand to people to continue their occupations.

" I always escape to places where I can hear English tongues, and I wanted to congratulate Madame on her reception yesterday, also to present to her my cousin Prince Rupert, who arrived this afternoon."

Prince Rupert and some of the wiser and more politic gentlemen, Eustace among them, drew apart in consultation, while the Prince of Wales stood by me.

" They are considering of a descent on the Isle of Wight to carry off my father from Carisbrooke," he said.

" And will not your Highness be with them ? " I asked.

" Oh yes, I shall be with them, of course, as soon as there is anything to be done; but as to the ways and means, they may arrange that as they choose. Are you to be at Madame de Choisy's ball ? "

I was quite provoked with him for being able to think of such matters when his father's rescue was at stake ; but he bade me ask his mother and mine whether it were not an important question, and then told me that he must make me understand the little comedy in which he was an actor.

Prince as he was, I could not help saying that I cared more for the tragedy in which we all might be actors ; and he shrugged his shoulders, and said that life would be insupportable if all were to be taken in the grand serious way. However, Prince Rupert appealed to him, and he was soon absorbed into the consultation.

My brother told us the next morning of the plan. It
was that Prince Rupert, with the ships which he had in
waiting at Harfleur, should take a trusty band of cavaliers
from Paris, surprise Carisbrooke, and carry off His Sacred
Majesty.   Eustace was eager to go with them, and would
listen to no representations from my mother of the danger
his health would incur in such an expedition in the month
of November.   She wept and entreated in vain.

"What was his life good for," he said, " but to be
given for the King's service ? "

Then she appealed to me to persuade him, but he
looked at me with his bright blue eyes and said:

"Meg learned better in Lorraine;" and I went up
and kissed him with tears in my eyes, and said: "Ah!
Madame, we have all had to learn how loyalty must
come before life, and what is better than life."

And then Annora cried out: "Well said, Margaret!
I do believe that you are an honest Englishwoman
still."

My brother went his way to consult with some of
the other volunteers, and my mother called for her sedan
chair to go and see whether she could get an order from
Queen Henrietta to stop him, while Annora exclaimed:

"Yes! I know how it is, and mother cannot see it.
Eustace cares little for his life now, and the only chance
of his ever overgetting it is the having something to do.
How can he forget while he lives moping here in banish-

ment, with nothing better to do than to stroke the
Queen's spaniels ? "

Then of course I asked what he had to get over.   I
knew he had had a boyish admiration for Millicent Wardour, a young lady in Lady Northumberland's household,
but I had never dared inquire after her, having heard
nothing about her since I left England.   My sister,
whose mistrust of me had quite given way, told me all
she knew.

Eustace had prevailed on my father to make proposals
of marriage for her, though not willingly, for my father
did not like the politics of her father, Sir James Wardour,
and my mother did not think the young gentlewoman a
sufficient match for the heir of Walwyn and Ribaumont.
There was much haggling over the dowry and marriage
portion, and in the midst, Sir James himself took, for his
second wife, a stern and sour Puritan dame.   My mother
and she were so utterly alien to each other that they
affronted one another on their first introduction, and Sir
James entirely surrendered himself to his new wife ; the
match was broken off, and Millicent was carried away
into the country, having returned the ring and all other
tokens that Eustace had given her.

" I never esteemed her much," said Nan. · " She was
a poor little white, spiritless thing, with a skin that they
called ivory, and great brown eyes that looked at one
like that young fawn with the broken leg.   If I had

been Eustace, I would have had some one with a little more will of her own, and then he would not have been served as he was." For the next thing that was heard of her, and that by a mere chance, was that she was married to Mynheer van Hunker, " a rascallion of an old half-bred Dutchman," as my hot-tongued sister called him, who had come over to fatten on our misfortunes by buying up the cavaliers' plate and jewels, and lending them money on their estates. He was of noble birth, too, if a Dutchman could be, and he had an English mother, so he pretended to be doing people a favour while he was filling his own coffers; and, worst of all, it was he who had bought the chaplet of pearls, the King's gift to the bravest of knights.

The tidings were heard in the midst of war and confusion, and, so far as Nan knew, Eustace had made no moan; but some months later, when he was seeking a friend among the slain at Cropredy Bridge, he came upon Sir James Wardour mortally wounded, to whom he gave some drink, and all the succour that was possible. The dying man looked up and said: "Mr. Rib'mont, I think. Ah! sir, you were scurvily used. My lady would have her way. My love to my poor wench; I wish she were in your keeping, but——" Then he gave some message for them both, and, with wandering senses, pained Eustace intensely by forgetting that he was not indeed Millicent's husband, and talking to him as such, giving the last greetings; and so he died in my brother's arms.

Eustace wrote all that needed to be said, and sent the letters, with the purse and tokens that Sir James had given him for them, with a flag of truce to the enemy's camp.

Then came still darker days—my father's death at Marston Moor, the year of losses, and Eustace's wound at Naseby, and his illness almost to death. When he was recovering, Harry Merrycourt, to whom he had given his parole, was bound to take him to London for his trial, riding by easy stages as he could endure it, whilst Harry took as much care of him as if he had been his brother. On the Saturday they were to halt over the Sunday at the castle of my Lord Hartwell, who had always been a notorious Roundhead, having been one of the first to take the Covenant.

Being very strong, and the neighbourhood being mostly of the Roundhead mind, his castle had been used as a place of security by many of the gentry of the Parliamentary party while the Royal forces were near, and they had not yet entirely dispersed, so that the place overflowed with guests; and when Harry and Eustace came down to supper, they found the hall full of company. Lord Walwyn was received as if he were simply a guest. While he was being presented to the hostess on coming down to supper, there was a low cry, then a confusion among the ladies, round some one who had fainted.

"The foolish moppet," said my unmerciful sister, "to expose herself and poor Walwyn in that way!"

I pitied her, and said that she could not help it.

"I would have run my finger through with my bodkin sooner than have made such a fool of myself," returned Nan. "And to make it worse, what should come rolling to my poor brother's feet but three or four of our pearls? The pearls of Ribaumont! That was the way she kept them when she had got them, letting the string break, so that they rolled about the floor anyhow!"

She had heard all this from Harry Merrycourt, and also that my brother had gathered up the pearls, and, with some other gentlemen, who had picked them up while the poor lady was carried from the room, had given them to my Lady Hartwell to be returned to Madame van Hunker, not of course escaping the remark from some of the stricter sort that it was a lesson against the being adorned with pearls and costly array.

Madame van Hunker's swoon had not surprised any one, for she was known to have been in very delicate health ever since a severe illness which she had gone through in London. She had been too weak to accompany her husband to Holland, and he had left her under the care of Lady Hartwell, who was a kinswoman of her own. Harry had only seen her again at supper time the next day, when he marvelled at the suffering such a pale little insignificant faded being could cause

Eustace, who, though silent and resolute, was, in the eyes of one who knew him well—evidently enduring a great trial with difficulty.

I heard the rest from my brother himself.

He was in no condition to attend the service the next day, not being able to walk to the Church, nor to sit and stand in the draughty building through the prayer and preaching that were not easily distinguished from one another. He was glad of such a dispensation without offence, for, children, though you suppose all Protestants to be alike, such members of the English Church as my family stand as far apart from the sects that distracted England as we do from the Huguenots; and it was almost as much against my brother's conscience to join in their worship, as it would be against our own. The English Church claims to be a branch of the true Catholic Church, and there are those among the Gallicans who are ready to admit her claim.

Harry Merrycourt, who was altogether a political, not a religious rebel, would gladly have kept Lord Walwyn company; but it was needful not to expose himself to the suspicion of his hosts, who would have bestowed numerous strange names on him had he absented himself.

And thus Eustace was left alone in the great hall, lord and lady, guests and soldiers, men and maids, all going off in procession across the fields; while he had his

choice of the cushions in the sunny window, or of the
large arm-chair by the wood fire on the hearth.

All alone there he had taken out his Prayer-book,
a little black clasped book with my father's coat-of-arms
and one blood-stain on it—he loved it as we love our
Book of the Hours, and indeed, it is much the very same,
for which reason it was then forbidden in England—and
was kneeling in prayer, joining in spirit with the rest of
his Church, when a soft step and a rustle of garments
made him look up, and he beheld the white face and
trembling figure of poor Millicent.

"Sir," she said, as he rose, "I ask your pardon. I
should not have interrupted your devotions, but now is
your time. My servant's riding-dress is in a closet by
the buttery hatch, his horse is in the stable, there is no
sentry in the way, for I have looked all about. No one
will return to the house for at least two hours longer ;
you will have full time to escape."

I can see the smile of sadness with which my brother
looked into her face as he thanked her, and told her that
he was on his parole of honour. At that answer she
sank down into a chair, hiding her face and weeping—
weeping with such an agony of self-abandonment and
grief as rent my brother's very heart, while he stood in
grievous perplexity, unable to leave her alone in her
sorrow, yet loving her too well and truly to dare to console her. One or two broken words made him think she

feared for his life, and he made haste to assure her that
it was in no danger, since Mr. Merrycourt was assured of
bearing him safely through. She only moaned in answer,
and said presently something about living with such a
sort of people as made her forget what a cavalier's truth
and honour were.

He was sorely shaken, but he thought the best and
kindest mode of helping her to recover herself would be
to go on where he was in the morning prayer, and, being
just in the midst of their Litany, he told her so, and
read it aloud. She knelt with her head on the cushions
and presently sobbed out a response, growing calmer as
he went on.

When it was ended she had ceased weeping, though
Eustace said it was piteous to see how changed she was,
and the startled pleading look in the dark eyes that used
to look at him with such confiding love.

She said she had not heard those prayers since one
day in the spring, when she had stolen out to a house in
town where there was a gathering round one of the per-
secuted ministers, and alas! her stepdaughters had suspected her, and accused her to their father. He pursued
her, caused the train-bands to break in on the congregation
and the minister to be carried off to prison. It was this
that had brought on the sickness of which she declared
that she hoped to have died.

When Eustace would have argued against this wish,

it brought out all that he would fain never have heard
nor known.

The poor young thing wished him to understand that
she had never been untrue to him in heart, as indeed was
but too plain, and she had only withdrawn her helpless
passive resistance to the marriage with Mr. Van Hunker
when Berenger's death had (perhaps wilfully) been reported to her as that of Eustace de Ribaumont. She
had not known him to be alive till she had seen him the
day before. Deaths in her own family had made her an
heiress sufficiently well endowed to excite Van Hunker's
cupidity, but he had never affected much tenderness for
her. He was greatly her elder, she was his second wife,
and he had grown-up daughters who made no secret of
their dislike and scorn. Her timid drooping ways and
her Royalist sympathies offended her husband, shown up
before him as they were by his daughters, and, in short,
her life had been utterly miserable. Probably, as Annora
said, she had been wanting in spirit to rise to her situation, but of course that was not as my brother saw it.
He only beheld what he would have cherished torn from
him only to be crushed and flung aside at his very feet, yet
so that honour and duty forbade him to do anything for her.

What he said, or what comfort he gave her, I do not
fully know, for when he confided to me what grief it was
that lay so heavily on his heart and spirits, he dwelt more
on her sad situation than on anything else. The belief

in her weakness and inconstancy had evoked in him a spirit of defiance and resistance ; but when she was proved guiltless and unhappy, the burden, though less bitter, was far heavier.   I only gathered that he, as the only like-minded adviser she had seen for so long, had felt it his duty to force himself to seem almost hard, cold, and pitiless in the counsel he gave her.

I remember his very words as he writhed himself with the pain of remembrance : " And then, Meg, I had to treat the poor child as if I were a mere stone of ada-mant, and chide her when my very heart was breaking for her.   One moment's softening, and where should we have been ?   And now I have added to her troubles that fancy that I was obdurate in my anger and implaca-bility."   I assured him that she would honour and thank him in her heart for not having been weak, and he began to repent of what he had left to be inferred, and to assure me of his having neither said nor done anything that could be censured, with vehement laudation of her sweet-ness and modesty.

The interview had been broken up by the sight of the return from Church.   Mrs. Van Hunker had had full time to retire to her room and Eustace to arrange him-self, so that no one guessed at the visitor he had had. She came down to supper, and a few words and civilities had passed between them, but he had never either seen or heard of her since.

Harry Merrycourt, who had known of the early passages between them, had never guessed that there was more than the encounter in the hall to cause the melancholy which he kindly watched and bore with in my brother, who was seriously ill again after he reached their lodgings in London, and indeed I thought at the time when he was with me in Paris, that his decay of health chiefly proceeded from sorrow of heart.

CHAPTER XIII.

MADEMOISELLE'S TOILETTE.

WE were to go to Madame de Choisy's assembly. She was the wife of the Chanceller of the Duke of Orleans, and gave a *fête* every year, to which all the court went; and, by way of disarming suspicion, all the cavaliers who were in the great world were to attend in order that their plans might not be suspected.

Our kind Queen Henrietta insisted on inspecting Nan and me before we went. She was delighted with the way in which my mother had dressed our hair, made her show how it was done, and declared it was exactly what was suited to her niece, Mademoiselle, none of whose women had the least notion of hairdressing. She was going herself to the Luxembourg to put the finishing touches, and Nan and I must come with her. I privately thought my mother would have been more to the purpose, but the Queen wanted to show the effect of the handi-work. However, Nan disliked the notion very much, and showed it so plainly in her face that the Queen

exclaimed : " You are no courtier, Mademoiselle de
Ribaumont. Why did you not marry her to her
Roundhead cousin, and leave her in England, Madame ?
Come, my god-daughter, you at least have learnt the art
of commanding your looks."

Poor Annora must have had a sad time of it with my
mother when we were gone. She was a good girl, but
she had grown up in rough times, and had a proud independent nature that chafed and checked at trifles, and
could not brook being treated like a hairdresser's block,
even by Queens and Princesses. She was likewise very
young, and she would have been angered instead of
amused at the scene which followed, which makes me
laugh whenever I think of it.

The Queen sent messages to know whether the Prince
of Wales were ready, and presently he came down in a
black velvet suit slashed with white and carnation ribbons,
and a little enamelled jewel on his gold chain, represent-
ing a goose of these three colours. His mother turned
him all round, smoothed his hair, fresh buckled his plume,
and admonished him with earnest entreaties to do himself
credit.

" I will, Madame," he said. " I will do my very
utmost to be worthy of my badge."

" Now, Charles, if you play the fool and lose her, I
will never forgive you."

I understood it soon. The Queen was bent on winning for her son the hand of Mademoiselle, a grand-daughter of France, and the greatest heiress there. If all were indeed lost in England, he would thus be far from a landless Prince, and her wealth might become a great assistance to the royal cause in England. But Mademoiselle was several years older than the Prince, and was besides stiff, haughty, conceited, and not much to his taste, so he answered rather sullenly that he could not speak French.

"So much the better," said his mother; "you would only be uttering follies. When I am not there, Rupert must speak for you."

"Rupert is too High-Dutch to be much of a courtier," said the Prince.

"Rupert is old enough to know what is for your good, and not sacrifice all to a jest," returned his mother.

By this time the carriage had reached the Palais Royal. We were told that Mademoiselle was still at her toilette, and up we all went, through ranks of Swiss and lackeys, to her apartments, to a splendid dressing-room, where the Princess sat in a carnation dress, richly ornamented with black and white, all complete except the fastening the feather in her hair. The *friseur* was engaged in this critical operation, and whole ranks of ladies stood round, one of them reading aloud one of *Plutarch's Lives*. The Queen came forward, with the most perfect grace, crying: "Oh, it is ravishing!"

What a coincidence!" and pointing to her son, as if the
similarity in colours had been a mere chance instead of a
contrivance of hers.

Then, with the most gracious deference in the world,
so as not to hurt the hairdresser's feelings, she showed
my head, and begged permission to touch up her niece's,
kissing her as she did so. Then she signed to the
Prince to hold her little hand-mirror, and he obeyed,
kneeling on one knee before Mademoiselle; while the
Queen, with hands that really were more dexterous than
those of any one I ever saw, excepting my mother, dealt
with her niece's hair, paying compliments in her son's
name all the time, and keeping him in check with her
eye. She contrived to work in some of her own jewels,
rubies and diamonds, to match the scarlet, black, and
white. I have since found the scene mentioned in Mademoiselle's own memoirs, but she did not see a quarter of
the humour of it. She was serene in the certainty that
her aunt was paying court to her, and the assurance that
her cousin was doing the same, though she explains that,
having hopes of the Emperor, and thinking the Prince a
mere landless exile, she only pitied him. Little did she
guess how he laughed at her, his mother, and himself,
most of all at her airs, while his mother, scolding him all
the time, joined in the laugh, though she always main-
tained that Mademoiselle, in spite of her overweening
conceit and vanity, would become an excellent and

faithful wife, and make her husband's interests her
own.

"Rather too much so," said the Prince, shrugging his
shoulders; "we know what the Margaret of Anjou style
of wife can do for a King of England."

However, as he always did what any one teased him
about, if it were not too unpleasant, and as he was passionately fond of his mother, and was amused by playing
on the vanity of *la grande Mademoiselle*, he acted his part
capitally. It was all in dumb show, for he really could
not speak French at that time, though he could understand
what was said to him. He, like a good many other
Englishmen, held that the less they assimilated themselves
to their French hosts, the more they showed their hopes
of returning home, and it was not till after his expedition
to Scotland that he set himself to learn the language.

Queen Henrietta's skill in the toilette was noted.
She laughingly said that if everything else failed her
she should go into business as a hairdresser, and she
had hardly completed her work, before a message was
brought from Queen Anne to desire to see Mademoiselle
in her full dress.

I do not know what would have become of me, if my
good-natured royal godmother, who never forgot anybody,
had not packed me into a carriage with some of the ladies
who were accompanying Mademoiselle. That lady had a
suite of her own, and went about quite independently of

her father and her stepmother, who, though a Princess of Lorraine, was greatly contemned and slighted by the proud heiress.

I was put *au courant* with all this by the chatter of the ladies in the coach. I did not know them, and in the dark they hardly knew who was there. Men with flambeaux ran by the side of the carriage, and now and then the glare fell across a smiling face, glanced on a satin dress, or gleamed back from some jewels; and then we had a long halt in the court of the Tuileries, while Mademoiselle went to the Queen-Regent to be inspected. We waited a long time, and I heard a great deal of gossip before we were again set in motion, and when once off we soon found ourselves in the court of the Hôtel de Choisy, where we mounted the stairs in the rear of Mademoiselle, pausing on the way through the anteroom, in order to give a final adjustment to her head-dress before a large mirror, the Prince of Wales standing obediently beside her, waiting to hand her into the room, so that the two black, white, and carnation figures were reflected side by side, which was, I verily believe, the true reason of her stopping there, for Queen Henrietta's handiwork was too skilful to require retouching. Prince Rupert was close by, to act as interpreter, his tall, powerful figure towering above them both, and his dark eyes looking as if his thoughts were far off, yet keeping in control the young Prince's great inclination to grimace and otherwise make game of Mademoiselle's magnificent affectations and condescensions.

I was rather at a loss, for the grand *salon* was one sea of feathers, bright satins and velvets, and curled heads, and though I tried to come in with Mademoiselle's suite I did not properly belong to it, and my own party were entirely lost to me. I knew hardly any one, and was quite unaccustomed to the great world, so that, though the Princess's *dame de compagnie* was very kind, I seemed to belong to no one in that great room, where the ladies were sitting in long rows, and the gentlemen parading before them, paying their court to one after another, while the space in the middle was left free for some distinguished pair to dance the *menuet de la cour.*

The first person I saw, whom I knew, was the Duchess of Longueville, more beautiful than when I had met her before as Mademoiselle de Bourbon, perfectly dazzling, indeed, with her majestic bearing and exquisite complexion, but the face had entirely lost that innocent, wistful expression that had so much enchanted me before. Half a dozen gentlemen were buzzing round her, and though I once caught her eye she did not know me, and no wonder, for I was much more changed than she was. However, there I stood forlorn, in an access of English shyness, not daring to take a chair near any of the strangers, and looking in vain for my mother or one of my brothers.

"Will not Madame take a seat beside me?" said a
kind voice. "I think I have had the honour of making
her acquaintance," she added, as our eyes met; "it is
the Gildippe of happier times."

Then I knew her for Mademoiselle d'Argennes, now
Duchess of Montausier, the same who had been so kind
to me at the Hôtel de Rambouillet on my first arrival at
Paris. Most gladly did I take my seat by her as an old
friend, and I learned from her that her mother was not
present, and she engaged me to go and see her at the
Hôtel de Rambouillet the next morning, telling me that
M. de Solivet had spoken of me, and that Madame de
Rambouillet much wished to see me. Then she kindly
told me the names of many of the persons present, among
whom were more *gens de la robe* than it was usual for us
of the old nobility to meet. They were indeed ennobled,
and thus had no imposts to pay, but that did not put
them on a level with the children of crusaders. So said
my mother and her friends, but I could not but be struck
with the fine countenance and grave collected air of the
President Mathieu de Molé, who was making his bow
to the hostess.

Presently, in the violet robes of a Bishop, for which
he looked much too young, there strolled up a keen-faced
man with satirical eyes, whom Madame de Montausier
presented as "Monseigneur le Coadjuteur." This was
the Archbishop of Corinth, Paul de Gondi, Coadjutor to

his uncle, the Archbishop of Paris. I think he was the most amusing talker I ever heard, only there was a great spice of malice in all that he said—or did not say ; and Madame de Montausier kept him in check, as she well knew how to do.

At last, to my great joy, I saw my brother walking with a young man in the black dress of an advocate. He came up to me, and the Duchess bade me present him, declaring herself delighted to make the acquaintance of a brave English cavalier, and at the same time greeting his companion as Monsieur Darpent. Eustace presently said that my mother had sent him in quest of me, and he conducted me through the *salon* to another apartment, where the ladies, as before, sat with their backs to the wall, excepting those who were at card-tables, a party having been made up for *Monsieur.* On my way I was struck both with the good mien and good sense of the young lawyer, who still stood conversing with my brother after I had been restored to my mother. The cloud cleared up from Annora's face as she listened, making her look as lovely and as animated as when she was in English company. The conversation was not by any means equally pleasing to my mother, who, on the first opportunity, broke in with "My son," and sent my brother off in search of some distinguished person to whom she wished to speak, and she most expressingly frowned off his former companion, who would have con-

tinued the conversation with my sister and me, whereupon Nan's face, which was always far too like a window,
became once more gloomy.

When we went home, it appeared that my mother
was well satisfied that I should be invited to the Hôtel
de Rambouillet. It was a distinguished thing to have
the *entrée* there, though for her part she thought it very
wearisome to have to listen to declamations about she
knew not what; and there was no proper distinction of
ranks kept up, any more than at the Hôtel de Choisy,
where one expected it. And, after all, neither Monsieur
nor Madame de Rambouillet were of the old *noblesse*.
The Argennes, like the Rambouillets, only dated from
the time of the League, when they had in private con-
firmed the sentence of death on the Duke of Guise,
which had been carried out by his assassination. Strange
to look at the beautiful and gentle Julie, and know her
to be sprung from such a stem!

Then my mother censured Eustace for bad taste in
talking over his case with his lawyer in public. He
laughed, and assured her that he had never even thought
of his suit, but had been discussing one of the pictures
on the walls, a fine Veronese—appealing to me if it were
not so; but she was not satisfied; she said he should
not have encouraged the presumption of that little
advocate by presenting him to his sisters.

Eustace never attempted argument with her, but went

his own way; and when Annora broke out with something about Mr. Hyde and other lawyers, such as Harry Merry-court, being company for any one in London, she was instantly silenced for presuming to argue with her elders.

I had a happy morning with Mesdames de Ram-bouillet and De Montausier, who showed the perfect union of mother and daughter.

In the little cabinet where Madame de Rambouillet read and studied so much in order to be able to fill her eminent position, she drew out from me all my story and all my perplexities, giving me advice as a wise woman of my own Church alone could do, and showing me how much I might still do in my life at Paris. She advised me, as I had been put under Father Vincent's guidance, to seek him at the Church of St. Sulpice, where, on certain days of the week, he was accessible to ladies wishing to under-take pious works. For the rest, she said that a little resolution on my part would enable me to reserve the early part of the day for study and the education of my son; and she fully approved of my giving the evenings to society, and gave me at once the *entrée* to her circle. She insisted that I should remain on that day and dine with her, and Madame de Montausier indited two charm-ing billets, which were sent to invite our family to join us there in the evening.

"It will not be a full circle," she said; "but I think

your brother treats as a friend a young man who is there to make his first *essai.*"

"M. Darpent?" I asked; and I was told that I was right, and that the young advocate had been writing a discourse upon Cicero which he was to read aloud to the fair critics and their friends. Madame de Montausier added that his father was a counsellor in the Parliament, who had originally been a Huguenot, but had converted himself with all his family, and had since held several good ,appointments. She thought the young man, Clé-ment Darpent, likely to become a man of mark, and she did not like him the less for having retained something of the Huguenot gravity.

The dinner was extremely pleasant; we followed it up by a walk in the beautifully laid out gardens; and after we had rested, the reception began, but only in the little green cabinet, as it was merely a select few who were to be admitted to hear the young aspirant. I watched anxiously for the appearance of my family, and presently in came Eustace and Annora. My mother had the *migraine,* and my brother had taken upon him, without asking leave, to carry off my sister!

I had never seen her look so well as she did, with that little spirit of mischief upon her, lighting her beau-tiful eyes and colouring her cheeks. Madame de Ram-bouillet whispered to me that she was a perfect nymph, with her look of health and freshness. Then M. Darpent

came in, and his grave face blushed with satisfaction as
he saw his friend, my Lord Walwyn, present.

His was a fine face, though too serious for so young
a man. It was a complete oval, the hair growing back
on the forehead, and the beard being dark and pointed,
the complexion a clear pale brown, the eyes with something of Italian softness in them, rather than of French
vivacity, the brows almost as if drawn with a pencil, the
mouth very grave and thoughtful except when lighted
by a smile of unusual sweetness. As a lawyer, his dress
was of plain black with a little white collar fastened by
two silken tassels (such as I remember my Lord Falk-
land used to wear). It became him better than the gay
coats of some of our nobles.

The circle being complete by this time, the young
orator was placed in the midst, and began to read aloud
his manuscript, or rather to recite it, for after the fire of
his subject began to animate him, he seldom looked at
the paper.

It was altogether a grand and eloquent discourse
upon the loyalty and nobility of holding with unswerving
faith to the old laws and constitutions of one's country
against all fraud, oppression, and wrong, tracing how
Cicero's weak and vain character grew stronger at the
call of patriotism, and how eagerly and bravely the once
timid man finally held out his throat for the knife. It
might be taken as the very highest witness to the manner

in which he had used his divine gift of rhetoric, that
Fulvia's first thought was to show her bitter hatred by
piercing his eloquent tongue! "Yes, my friends," he
concluded, with his eyes glancing round, "that insult to
the dead was the tribute of tyranny to virtue!"

Annora's hands were clasped, her cheeks were flushed,
her eyes glanced with the dew of admiration, and there
were others who were carried along by the charm of the
young orator's voice and enthusiasm; but there were also
anxious glances passing, especially between the divine
Arthenice and her son-in-law, M. de Montausier, and
when there had been time for the compliments the discourse merited to be freely given, Madame de Rambouillet
said : "My dear friend, the tribute may be indeed the
highest, but it can scarcely be the most appreciable
either by the fortunate individual or his friends. I
therefore entreat that the most eloquent discourse of
our youthful Cicero may remain a valued secret among
the sincere circle of admirers who have listened
to it."

Everybody bowed assent, but the young man himself
began, with some impetuosity : "Madame will believe me
that I had not the slightest political intention. I spoke
simply as a matter of history."

"I am perfectly aware of it, Monsieur," returned the
Marquise; "but all the world does not understand as well
as I do how one may be carried away by the fervour of

imagination to identify oneself and one's surroundings with those of which one speaks."

" Madame is very severe on the absent," said M. Darpent.

" Monsieur thinks I have inferred more treason than he has spoken," said Madame de Rambouillet gaily. " Well, be it so ; I am an old woman, and you, my friend, have your career yet to come, and I would have you remember that though the great Cæsar be dead, yet the bodkin was not in his time."

" I understand, Madame, after the lion comes the fox. I thank you for your warning until the time——"

" Come, come, we do not intend to be all undone in the meantime," exclaimed Madame de Rambouillet. " Come, who will give us a *vaudeville* or something joyous to put out the grand serious, and send us home gay ? My dear Countess," and she turned to a bright-looking young lady, " relate to us, I entreat of you, one of your charming fairy tales."

And the Countess d'Aulnoy, at her request, seated herself in a large arm-chair, and told us with infinite grace the story I have so often told you, my grand-children, of the White Cat and the three Princes.

CHAPTER XIV.

COURT APPOINTMENT.

THE expected descent on the Isle of Wight did not take
place, for though Prince Rupert was High Admiral, so
large a portion of the fleet was disaffected that it was
not possible to effect anything. Before long, he went
back to the ships he had at Helvoetsluys, taking the
Prince of Wales with him. My brother Walwyn yielded
to an earnest entreaty that he would let us take care of
him at Paris till there was some undertaking really in hand.
Besides, he was awaiting the issue of his cause respecting
the Ribaumont property in Picardy, to which the Count
de Poligny set up a claim in right of a grant by King
Henry III. in the time of the League. It must be confessed that the suit lingered a good deal, in spite of the
zeal of the young advocate, M. Clément Darpent,—
nay, my mother and my brother De Solivet sometimes
declared, because of his zeal; for the Darpent family
were well known as inclined to the Fronde party.

They had been Huguenots, but had joined the Church

some twenty years before, as it was said, because of the
increased disabilities of Huguenots in the legal profession,
and it was averred that much of the factious Calvinist
leaven still hung about them. At this time I never
saw the parents, but Eustace had contracted a warm
friendship with the son, and often went to their house.
My mother fretted over this friendship far more, as
Annora used to declare, than if he had been intimate
with the wildest of the roystering cavaliers, or the most
dissipated of the *petits maîtres* of Paris. But Eustace
was a man now, made older than his twenty-five years
by what he had undergone, and though always most
respectful to my mother, he could not but follow his own
judgment and form his own friendships. And my
mother's dislike to having Clément Darpent at the Hôtel
de Nidemerle only led to Walwyn's frequenting the Maison
Darpent more than he might have done if he could have
seen his friend at home without vexing her.

I do not think that he much liked the old Counsellor,
but he used to say that Madame Darpent was one of the
most saintly beings he had ever seen. She had one married
daughter, and two more, nuns at Port Royal, and she was
with them in heart, the element of Augustinianism in the
Jansenist teaching having found a responsive chord in her
soul from her Calvinist education. She spent her whole
time, even while living in the world, in prayers, pious
exercises, and works of charity, and she would fain have

induced her son to quit secular life and become one of those recluses who inhabited the environs of Port Royal, and gave themselves to labour of mind and of hand, producing works of devotion and sacred research, and likewise making a paradise of the dreary unwholesome swamp in which stood Port Royal des Champs. Clément Darpent had, however, no vocation for such a life, or rather he was not convinced in his own mind that it was expedient for him. He was eight or nine years old when the conversion of his family had taken place, and his mother had taught him carefully her original faith. Her conversion had been, no one could doubt, most hearty and sincere, and her children had gone with her in all simplicity; but the seeds she had previously sown in her son's mind sprang up as he grew older, and when Eustace became his friend, he was, though outwardly conforming, restless and dissatisfied, by no means disposed to return to Calvinism, and yet with too much of the old leaven in him to remain contented in the Church. He was in danger of throwing off all thought of the faith and of Divine things in his perplexity, and I know many of our advisers would say this was best, provided he died at last in the bosom of the Catholic Church; but I can never think so, and, as things stood, Eustace's advice aided him in remaining at that time where he was, a member of the Church. My brother himself was, my mother ardently hoped, likely to join our communion. The Abbé Walter Montagu, who had himself been a convert, strove hard to win him over, trying to prove to him that the English Church was extinct, stifled by her own rebellious heretic children, so soon as the grace that was left in her began to work so as to bring her back to Catholic doctrine and practice. His argument was effectual with many of our fugitives, but not with my brother. He continued still to declare that he believed that his Church was in the course of being purified, and would be raised up again at last; and his heart was too loyal to desert her, any more than his King, because of her misfortunes. No one shall ever make me believe that he was wrong. As to Annora, I believe she would rather have been a Huguenot outright than one of us, and she only half trusted me for a long time.

We had begun to settle down into regular habits; indeed, except for the evenings, our days were almost more alike than when in the country. I had gone, as Madame de Rambouillet had advised me, to Father Vincent, and he introduced me to the excellent Madame Goussault, who had the sweetest old face I ever saw. She made me a member of the society for attending the poor in the Hôtel Dieu, and my regular days were set apart, twice a week, for waiting on the sick. We all wore a uniform dress of dark stuff, with a white apron and tight white cap, and, unless we were very intimate, were not supposed to recognise one another.

There was good reason for this. At the next bed to that of my patient there was a lady most tenderly, if a little awkwardly, bathing a poor man's face with essences. Her plump form, beautiful hands, and slightly Spanish accent, could only belong to one person, I thought, but I could hardly believe it, and I turned my eyes away, and tried the more diligently to teach my poor ignorant patient the meaning of his *Pater* and *Ave*, when suddenly there was a burst of scolding and imprecation from the other bed. The essence had gone into the man's eye, and he, a great rough *bûcheron*, was reviling the awkward-ness and meddling of ladies in no measured terms, while his nurse stood helplessly wringing her white hands, imploring his pardon, but quite unaware of what was to be done. Happily, I had a sponge and some warm water near, and I ran up with it and washed the man's eyes, while the lady thanked me fervently, but the man growled out :

" That is better; if women will come fussing over us with what they don't understand—— You are the right sort ; but for her——"

" Do not stop him," hastily said the lady, with her hand on my arm. " I love it ! I rejoice in it ! Do not deprive me, for the love of Heaven ! "

I knew who she was then, and Madame de Montausier told me I was right; but that I must keep the secret; and so I did, till after Queen Anne of Austria was dead.

She would not let her rank deprive her of the privilege of waiting on the poor, unknown and unthanked; and many hours, when those who blamed her for indolence supposed her to be in bed, she was attending the hospital.

Cécile was never strong enough to give her attendance there, but she made clothes which were given to the patients when they came out. We spent our mornings much as of old; the two elder children generally went to mass with me at St. Germain l'Auxerrois, and if the day were fine, I would take them for a few turns in the Tuileries Gardens afterwards before I taught them their little lessons, and gave my orders to the servants.

Then all the family met at breakfast, after which Gaspard had half an hour more of study with the Abbé, for he was beginning Latin, and was a very promising scholar. He prepared his tasks with me before breakfast, and got on admirably.

Then, unless I had to be at the hospital, we sat together at our embroidery—Cécile, Annora, and I—while the Abbé read to us. It was very hard to poor Nan to sit still, work, and listen. She had been used to such an active unsettled life during the war, and had been put to so many shifts, having at times for months together to do servant's work, that she knew not how to be quiet. Embroidery seemed to her useless, when she had cooked and washed, and made broths, and scraped lint for the wounded, and she could not care for the history of the

Romans, even when Eustace had given her his word they were not Roman Catholics.

She used to say she had the cramp, or that her foot was asleep, and rush off to play with the children, or to see if my mother wanted her. My mother did not care for the reading, but she did want Nan to learn to sit in her chair and embroider, like a *demoiselle bien élevée*, instead of a wild maiden of the civil wars. However, my mother spent most of her day in waiting on the Queen of England, who was very fond of her, and liked to have her at her *levée*, so that we really saw very little of her.

My brother, when not needed by his Queen, nor in consultation with the cavaliers, or with his lawyers, would often join in our morning's employment. He was not strong, and he liked to recline in a large chair that I kept ready for him, and listen while the Abbé read, or sometimes discuss with him questions that arose in the reading, and this was a great relief to Nan, who seldom declared that her feet tingled when he was there.

After our dinner we either walked in the garden where the children played, or went out to make visits. In the evening there were receptions. We had one evening to which, as I said, came our poor exiled country-men, and there were other assemblies, to some of which we went by invitation; but at the Hôtel de Rambouillet, and one or two others, we knew we were always welcome.

There we heard M. Corneille read the *Cid*, one of his finest pieces, before it was put on the stage. I cannot describe how those noble verses thrilled in our ears and hearts, how tears were shed and hands clasped, and how even Annora let herself be carried along by the tide. Clément Darpent was often there, and once or twice recited again, but Madame de Rambouillet always took care first to know what he was going to say. A poem upon St. Monica was the work of his that I liked best, but it was not so much admired as verses more concerned with the present.

The Prince of Condé came back to Paris for a few weeks, and my poor Cécile was greatly disappointed that her husband remained in garrison and did not come with him. " But then," as she said to console herself, " every month made the children prettier, and she was trying to be a little more nice and agreeable."

Two appointments were made for which I was less grateful than was my mother. My little son was made one of the King's gentlemen of the bedchamber, and Mademoiselle requested me to be one of her ladies-in-waiting. She was very good-natured, provided she thought herself obeyed, and she promised that my turn should always come at the same time as my son's, so that I might be at home with him. I was a little laughed at, and my former name of Gildippe was made to alternate with that of Cornelia ; but French mothers have always been devoted to their sons, and there was some sympathy with me among the ladies.

I owned that my presence was required at home, for Gaspard generally came back a much naughtier boy than he went, and with a collection of bad words that I had to proscribe. Before the Queen-Regent, the little King and the Duke of Anjou were the best boys in the world, and as stately and well-mannered as became the first gentlemen of France; but when once out of her sight they were the most riotous and mischievous children in the world, since nobody durst restrain, far less punish them. They made attacks on the departments of the stewards and cooks, kicking and biting any one who tried to stop them, and devouring fruit and sweetmeats till their fine clothes were all bedaubed, and they themselves indisposed, and then their poor valets suffered for it. The first time this happened my poor Gaspard was so much shocked that he actually told the King that it was dishonourable to let another suffer for his fault.

"I would have you to know, Monsieur le Marquis," said Louis XIV., drawing himself up, "that the King of France is never in fault."

However, I will say for His Majesty that it was the Duke of Anjou who told the Queen that the little Nidemerle had been disrespectful, and thus caused the poor child to be sent home, severely beaten, and with a reprimand to me for not bringing him up better.

I leave you to guess how furious I was, and how I raged about the house till I frightened my mother, Annora backing me up with all her might. We were almost ready to take Gaspard in our hands and escape at once to England. Even in its present sad state I should at least be able to bring up my boy without having him punished for honourable sentiments and brave speeches. Of course it was the Abbé on the one hand, and Eustace on the other, who moderated me, and tried to show me, as well as my son, that though the little Louis might be a naughty boy, the kingly dignity was to be respected in him.

" Thou wouldst not blame thy mother even if she were in fault," argued Eustace.

" But my mother never is in fault," said Gaspard, throwing himself into my arms.

" Ah, there spoke thy loyal heart, and a Frenchman should have the same spirit towards his King."

" Yes," broke out Annora ; " that is what you are all trying to force on your children, setting up an idol to fall down and crush yourselves ! For shame, Walwyn, that you, an Englishman, should preach such a doctrine to the poor child ! "

" Nay, you little Frondeuse, there is right and safety in making a child's tongue pay respect to dignities. He must separate the office from the man, or the child."

All that could be done was that I should write a

humble apology for my son. Otherwise they told me he
would certainly be taken from so dangerous a person,
and such a dread always made me submissive to the
bondage in which we were all held.

Was it not strange that a Queen who would with her
own hands minister to the sufferers in the hospital
should be so utterly ignorant of her duties in bringing
up the heir of a great kingdom ? Gaspard, who was
much younger, could read well, write, and knew a little
Latin and English, while the King and his brother were
as untaught as peasants in the fields. They could
make the sign of the cross and say their prayers, and
their manners *could* be perfect, but that was all. They
had no instruction, and their education was not begun.
I have the less hesitation in recording this, as the King
has evidently regretted it, and has given first his son,
then his grandsons, the most admirable masters, besides
having taken great pains with himself.

I suppose the Spanish dislike to instruction dominated
the Queen, and made her slow to inflict on her sons what
she so much disliked, and she was of course perfectly
ignorant of their misbehaviour.

I am sorry to say that Gaspard soon ceased to be shocked.
His aunt declared that he was becoming a loyal Frenchman
when he showed off his Louvre manners by kicking the
lackeys, pinching Armantine, and utterly refusing to learn
his lessons for the Abbé, declaring that he was Monsieur

le Marquis, and no one should interfere with him. Once
when he came home a day or two before me, he made
himself quite intolerable to the whole house, by insisting
on making Armantine and her little brother defend a
fortress on the top of the stairs, which he attacked with
the hard balls of silk and wool out of our work-baskets.
Annora tried to stop him, but only was kicked for her
pains. It was his *hôtel* he said, and he was master there,
and so he went on, though he had given poor Armantine
a black eye, and broken two panes of glass, till his uncle
came home, and came upon him with a stern " Gaspard !"
The boy began again with his being the Marquis and the
master, but Eustace put him down at once.

" Thou mayst be Marquis, but thou art not master of
this house, nor of thyself. Thou art not even a gentleman while thou actest thus. Go to thy room. We will
see what thy mother says to this."

Gaspard durst not struggle with his uncle, and went
off silent and sulky ; but Eustace had subdued him into
penitence before I came home. And I can hardly tell
how, but from that time the principle of loyalty to
the sovereign, without imitation of the person, seemed
to have been instilled into the child, so that I feel,
and I am sure he will agree with me, that I owe my
son, and he owes himself, to the influence of my dear
brother.

Had it not been for leaving him, my services to

Mademoiselle would have been altogether amusing. True, she was marvellously egotistical and conceited, but she was very good-natured, and liked to make those about her happy. Even to her stepmother and little sisters, whom she did not love, she was never unkind, though she lived entirely apart, and kept her own little court separately at the Louvre, and very odd things we did there.

Sometimes we were all dressed up as the gods and goddesses, she being always Minerva—unless as Diana she conducted us as her nymphs to the chase in the park at Versailles. Sometimes we were Mademoiselle Scudery's heroines, and we wrote descriptions of each other by these feigned names, some of which appear in her memoirs. And all the time she was hoping to marry the Emperor, and despising the suit of Queen Henrietta for our Prince of Wales, who, for his part, never laughed so much in secret as when he attended this wonderful and classical Court.

CHAPTER XV.

A STRANGE THANKSGIVING DAY.

THERE was a curious scene in our *salon* the day after the news had come of the great victory of Lens. Clément Darpent had been brought in by my brother, who wished him to hear some English songs which my sister and I had been practising. He had been trying to learn English, and perhaps understood it better than he could speak it, but he was somewhat perplexed by those two gallant lines—

> "I could not love thee, dear, so much,
> Loved I not honour more."

Annora's eyes flashed with disappointed anger as she said, "You enter not into the sentiment, Monsieur. I should have hoped that if any Frenchman could, it would be you !"

"For my part," observed my mother, "I am not surprised at the question not being appreciated by the *gens de la robe*."

I saw Eustace look infinitely annoyed at this insult
to his friend's profession, and to make it worse, Gaspard,
who had come home that morning from the palace,
exclaimed, having merely caught the word " honour "—

"Yes, the *gens de la robe* hate our honour. That is
why the King said, when news of our great victory came,
' Oh, how sorry the Parliament will be!' "

"Did he?" exclaimed my mother. "Is it true, my
grandson?"

"True; yes indeed, Madame ma Grandmère," replied
Gaspard. "And you should have seen how all the world
applauded him."

"I would not have applauded him," said Eustace
sadly. "I would have tried to teach him that nothing
can be of more sad omen for a king than to regard his
Parliament as his enemy."

"My son," returned my mother, "if you must utter
such absurdities, let it not be before the child. Imagine
the consequence of his repeating them!"

"Ah!" sighed Darpent, "it would be well if only,
through child lips or any others, the King and his mother
could learn that the Parliament can heartily rejoice in all
that is for the true glory of France; but that we place
that glory and honour in justice and in the well-being of
her people, and that we love above all!"

"There," said I, glad to turn the conversation from
the dangerous political turn it was taking, "I knew it

was merely the language and not the sentiment of our
song that Monsieur Darpent did not comprehend."

And when it was translated and paraphrased, he
exclaimed, " Ah ! truly Mademoiselle may trust me that
such sentiments are the breath of life to those who are
both French and of the robe. May *one* at least live to
prove it to her ! "

The times were threatening in France as well as in
England, for if in the latter realm the thunderbolt had
fallen, in the former the tempest seemed to be gathering.
They say that it dispersed after a few showers, but there
are others who say that it is only stored up to fall with
greater fury in later times. Ah, well! if it be so, I pray
that none of mine may be living to see it, for I cannot
conceal from myself that there is much among us that
may well call down the vengeance of Heaven. Yet, if
our good Duke of Burgundy fulfil the promise of his
youth, the evil may yet be averted.

The Parliament of Paris had made an attempt to
check the reckless exactions of the Court by refusing to
register the recent edicts for taxation, and it was this
that made the Queen so angry with them. Eustace began
to explain that it had been the unfortunate endeavour
to raise money without the consent of Parliament that
had been the immediate cause of the troubles in England
for which they were still suffering. This implied censure
of King Charles so displeased my mother that she declared

that she would listen to such treason no longer, started
up and quitted the room, calling Annora with her. Poor
Annora gave one of her grim looks, but was obliged to
obey ; I did not feel bound to do the same, as indeed
I stood in the position of hostess : so I remained, with
Gaspard leaning on my lap, while my brother and M.
Darpent continued their conversation, and the latter began
to describe the actual matter in debate, the Paulette,
namely, the right of magistrates to purchase the succession
to their offices for their sons, provided a certain annual
amount was paid to the Crown. The right had to be
continually renewed by fresh edicts for a certain term.
This term was now over, and the Crown refused to renew
it except on condition that all the salaries should be for-
feited for four years. To our English notions the whole
system was a corruption, but the horrible ill faith of the
Court, which ruined and cheated so many families, was
nevertheless shocking to us. Clément Darpent, who had
always looked on the Paulette as a useful guarantee, and
expected to succeed to his father's office as naturally as
Eustace had done to the baronies of Walwyn and Ribaumont, could not then see it in the same light, and expa-
tiated on the speeches made by the Councillors Broussel,
Blancmesnil, and others, on the injustice of such a
measure.

Gaspard caught the name of Blancmesnil, and looking up, he said " Blancmesnil ! It is he that the King

says is a scoundrel to resist his will; but he will soon be shut up. They are going to arrest him."

" Pray how long have they taken little imps like thee into their counsels ?" demanded Eustace, as we all sat petrified at this announcement.

" It was the Duke of Anjou who told me," said Gaspard. " He was sitting at the foot of the Queen's bed when she settled it all with M. le Cardinal. They will send to have *coup de main* made of all those rogues as soon as the *Te Deum* is over to-morrow at Notre Dame, and then there will be no more refusing of money for M. le Prince to beat the Spaniards with."

" The Duke should choose his confidants better," said Eustace. " Look here, my nephew. Remember from henceforth that whatever passes in secret council is sacred, and even if told to thee inadvertently should never be repeated. Now leave us; your mother needs you no longer."

My little boy made his graceful bow at the door, looking much perplexed, and departed. I rose likewise, saying I would forbid him to repeat his dangerous communication, and I trusted that it would do him no harm.

" Madame," said M. Darpent, " I will not conceal from you that I shall take advantage of what I have heard to warn these friends of my father."

" You cannot be expected to do otherwise," said Eustace ; " and truly the design is so arbitrary and unjust that, Cavalier as I am, I cannot but rejoice that it should be baffled."

" And," added Darpent, before I could speak, " Madame may be secure that no word shall pass my lips respecting the manner in which I received the warning."

I answered that I could trust him for that. I could not expect any more from him, and indeed none of us were bound in honour. The fault was with the Duke of Anjou, who, as we all know, was an incorrigible chatterbox all his life, and never was trusted with any State secrets at all ; but his mother must have supposed him not old enough to understand what she was talking about, when she let him overhear such a conversation.

Gaspard had, however, a private lecture from both of us on the need of holding his tongue, both on this matter and all other palace gossip. He was no longer in waiting, and I trusted that all would be forgotten before his turn came again ; but he was to join in the state procession on the following day, a Sunday, when the King and Queen-Regent were to return thanks at Notre Dame for the victory at Lens.

Ah, children ! we had victories then. Our *Te Deums* were not sung with doubting hearts, to make the populace believe a defeat a victory—a delusion to which this French nation of ours is only too prone. My countryman, Marlborough, and the little truant Abbé, Eugène of Savoy, were not then the leaders of the opposite armies ;

but at the head of our own, we had M. le Prince and the
Vicomte de Turenne in the flower of their age, and our
triumphs were such that they might well intoxicate the
King, who was, so to speak, brought up upon them. It
was a magnificent sight, which we all saw from different
quarters—my mother in the suite of the Queen of England,
Gaspard among the little noblemen who attended the
King, I among the ladies who followed Mademoiselle,
while my brother and sister, though they might have
gone among their own Queen's train, chose to shift for
themselves, They said they should see more than if,
like us, they formed part of the pageant; but I believe
the real reason was, that if they had gone early to Queen
Henrietta's apartments in full dress, they must have missed
their English prayers at the Ambassador's, which they
never chose to do on a Sunday.

The choir part of the nave was filled with tribunes
for the royal family and their suites; and as the most
exalted in rank went the last, Mademoiselle, and we ladies
behind her, came to our places early enough to see a great
deal of the rest of the procession. The whole choir was
already a field of clergy and choristers, the white robes of
the latter giving relief to the richly-embroidered purple
and lace-covered robes of the Bishops, who wore their gold
and jewelled mitres, while their richly-gilded pastoral
staves and crosses were borne before them. The Coadjutor of Paris, who was to be the Celebrant, was already

by the Altar, his robes absolutely encrusted with gold; and just after we had taken our places there passed up the Cardinal, with his pillars borne before him, in his scarlet hat and his robes.

Every lady was, according to the Spanish fashion, which Queen Anne had introduced, in black or in white— the demoiselles in white, the married in black—and all with the black lace veil on their heads. The French ladies had murmured much at this, but there is no denying that the general effect was much better for the long lines of black above and white below, and as there was no restriction upon their jewellery, emeralds, rubies, and diamonds flashed wherever the light fell on them.

Beyond, a lane was preserved all down the length of the nave by the tall, towering forms of the Scottish archers, in their rich accoutrements, many of them gallant gentlemen, who had served under the Marquess of Montrose; and in the aisles behind them surged the whole multitude—gentlemen, ladies, bourgeois, fishwives, artisans, all sorts of people, mixed up together, and treating one another with a civility and forbearance of which my brother and sister confessed an English crowd would have been incapable, though they showed absolutely no reverence to the sacred place; and I must own the ladies showed as little, for every one was talking, laughing, bowing to acquaintance, or pointing out notorieties, and low whispers were going about of some great and secret

undertaking of the Queen-Regent. Low, did I say!
Nay, I heard the words " Blancmesnil and Broussel "
quite loud enough to satisfy me that if the attempt had
been disclosed, it would not be possible to fix the blame
of betraying it on my little son more than on twenty
others. Indeed the Queen of England observed to her
niece, loud enough for me to hear her, that it was only
too like what she remembered only seven years ago in
England, when her dear King had gone down to arrest
those five rogues of members, and all had failed because
of that vile gossip Lady Carlisle.

" And who told my Lady Carlisle ? " demanded Mademoiselle with some archness ; whereupon Queen Henrietta became very curious to know whether the handsome
Duke of Beaufort were, after his foolish fashion, in the
crowd, making himself agreeable to the ladies of the
market-place.

Trumpets, however, sounded, and all rose from their
seats, as up the nave swept Queen Anne, her black man-
tilla descending over her fair hair from a little diamond
crown, her dress—white satin—with a huge long blue
velvet train worked with gold *fleurs-de-lys*, supported by
four pair of little pages in white satin. Most regal did
she look, leading by the hand the little Duke of Anjou ;
while the young King, who was now old enough to form
the climax of the procession, marched next after in blue
and gold, holding his plumed hat in his hand, and bowing

right and left with all his royal courtesy and grace, his beautiful fair hair on his shoulders, shining with the sun. And there was my little Marquis among the boys who immediately followed him in all his bright beauty and grace.

Most glorious was the High Mass that followed. Officer after officer marched up and laid standard after standard before the Altar, heavy with German blazonry, or with the red and gold stripes of Aragon, the embattled castles of Castille, till they amounted to seventy-three. It must have been strange to the Spanish Queen to rejoice over these as they lay piled in a gorgeous heap before the high Altar, here and there one dim with weather or stained with blood. The peals of the *Te Deum* from a thousand voices were unspeakably magnificent, and yet through them all it seemed to me that I heard the wail not only of the multitudes of widowed wives and sonless parents, but of the poor peasants of all the nation, crying aloud to Heaven for the bread which they were forbidden to eat, when they had toiled for it in the sweat of their brow. Yes, and which I was not permitted to let them enjoy!

Ah! which did the Almighty listen to? To the praise, or to the mourning, lamentation, and woe? You have often wondered, my children, that I absented myself from the *Te Deums* of victory while we had them. Now you know the reason.

And then I knew that all this display was only an

excuse under which the Queen hid her real design of crushing all opposition to her will. She wanted to commit an injustice, and silence all appeals against it, so that the poor might be more and more ground down! How strange in the woman whom I had seen bearing patiently, nay, joyfully, with the murmurs of the faggot-seller in the hospital! Truly she knew not what she did!

As she left the Cathedral, and passed M. de Comminges, a lieutenant of her Guards, she said: "Go, and Heaven be with you."

I was soon at home safely with my boys, to carry an account of our doings to my dear little Madame d'Aubépine, who, unable to bear the fatigue and the crush of Notre Dame, had taken her little children to a Mass of thanksgiving celebrated by our good Abbé at the nearest Church.

We waited long and long for the others to come. I was not uneasy for my mother, who was with the Queen; but the servants brought reports that the *canaille* had risen, and that the streets were in wild confusion. We could see nothing, and only heard wild shouts from time to time. What could have become of Eustace and Annora? My mother would have been afraid that with their wild English notions they had rushed into something most unsuitable to a French *demoiselle*, and I was afraid for Eustace, if they were involved in any crowd or confusion, for his strength was far from being equal to his spirit. We watched, sure that we heard cries and shouts in the distance, the roar of the populace, such as I remembered on that wedding day, but sharper and shriller, as French voices are in a different key from the English roar and growl.

It passed, however, and there was long silence. Gaspard and Armantine stood at the window, and at last, as evening twilight fell, cried out that a carriage was coming in at the *porte cochère*. Presently Annora rań into the room, all in a glow, and Eustace followed more slowly.

"Have you been frightened?" she cried. "Oh, we have had such an adventure! If they had not screamed and shrieked like peacocks, or furies, I could have thought myself in England."

"Alack! that a tumult should seem like home to you, sister," said Eustace gravely.

Then they told how at the ambassador's chapel they had heard that good Lady Fanshawe, whom they had known in England, had arrived sick and sad, after the loss of a young child. They determined, therefore, to steal away from Notre Dame before the ceremony was over, and go to see whether anything could be done for her. They could not, however, get out so quickly as they expected, and they were in the Rue des Marmousets when they saw surging towards them a tremendous crowd, shouting, screeching, shrieking, roaring, trying to stop a carriage which was being urged on with six horses, with the royal guards trying to force their way. Eustace, afraid of his sister being swept from him, looked for some escape, but the mob went faster than they could do; and they might soon have been involved in it and trampled down. There seemed no opening in the tall houses, when suddenly a little door opened close to them, and there was a cry of surprise; a hand was put out.

"You here! Nay, pardon me, Mademoiselle; take my arm."

Clément Darpent was there. A few steps more, and taking out a small key, he fitted it into the same little door, and led them into a dark passage, then up a stair, into a large room, simply furnished, and one end almost like an oratory. Here, looking anxiously from the window, was an old lady in a plain black dress and black silk hood, with a white apron and keys at her girdle.

"My mother," said Clément, "this gentleman and lady, M. le Baron de Ribaumont and Mademoiselle *sa sœur*, have become involved in this crowd. They will do us the favour of taking shelter here till the uproar is over."

Madame Darpent welcomed them kindly, but with anxious inquiries. Her son only threw her a word in answer, prayed to be excused, and dashed off again.

"Ah! there he is. May he be saved, the good old man," cried Madame Darpent.

And they could see a carriage with four horses con-
taining the Lieutenant Comminges holding a white-haired
old man, in a very shabby dressing-gown ; while soldiers,
men, women, boys, all struggled, fought, and shrieked
round it, like the furies let loose. The carriage passed
on, but the noise and struggle continued, and Madame
Darpent was soon intensely anxious about her son.

It seemed that Clément had carried his warnings,
and that four or five of the councillors had taken care
to be beyond the walls of Paris ; among them his own
father, the Councillor Darpent, who was a prudent man,
and thought it best to be on the right side. The President Blancmesnil was, however, absent each time Clément
had called to see him, and he durst not entrust his
message to any third person, nor write, as it now appeared
definitely enough to be understood. And the President
Broussel, a good-humoured, simple, hearty old man, was
not quite well, and though he thanked his young friend,
he would not believe any such harm was intended
against him as to make him derange his course of
medicine.

Thus, when Comminges marched into the house to
arrest him, he was sitting at dinner, eating his *bouillon*,
in dressing-gown and slippers. His daughter cried out
that he was not fit to leave the house. At the same
time, an old maid-servant put her head out at a window,
screaming that her master was going to be carried off.

He was much beloved, and a host of people ran together, trying to break the carriage and cut the traces. Comminges, seeing that no time was to be lost, forced the poor old lawyer down to the carriage just as he was, in his dressing-gown and slippers, and drove off. But the mob thickened every moment, in spite of the guards, and a very few yards beyond where they had taken refuge at Madame Darpent's, a large wooden bench had been thrown across the street, and the uproar redoubled round it—the yells, shrieks, and cries ringing all down the road. However, the carriage passed that, and dashed on, throwing down and crushing people right and left; so that Madame Darpent was first in terror for her son, and then would fain have rushed out to help the limping, crying sufferers.

They heard another horrible outcry, but could see no more, except the fluctuating heads of the throng below them, and loud yells, howls, and maledictions came to their ears. By and by, however, Clément returned, having lost his hat in the crowd; with blood on his collar, and with one of his lace cuffs torn, though he said he was not hurt.

"They have him!" he said bitterly; "the tyranny has succeeded!"

"Oh, hush, my son! Take care!" cried his mother.

"M. le Baron and I understand one another, Madame," he said, smiling.

He went on to tell that the carriage had been over-
turned on the Quai des Orfévres, just opposite the hotel
of the First President.   Comminges sprang out, sword in
hand, drove back the crowd, who would have helped out
Broussel, and shouted for the soldiers, some of whom
kept back those who would have succoured the prisoner
with their drawn swords.   Clément himself had been
slightly touched, but was forced back in the scuffle ;
while the good old man called out to him not to let any
one be hurt on his behalf.

Other soldiers were meantime seizing a passing carriage, and taking out a poor lady who occupied it.   Before
it could be brought near, the raging crowd had brought
axes and hacked it to pieces.   Comminges and his
soldiers, well armed, still dragged their victim along till
a troop of the Queen's guards came up with another
carriage, in which the poor old President was finally
carried off.

" And this is what we have to submit to from a
Spaniard and an Italian ! " cried Clément Darpent.

He had come back to reassure his mother and his
guests, but the tumult was raging higher than ever.   The
crowd had surrounded the Tuileries, filling the air with
shouts of " Broussel ! Broussel ! " and threatening to tear
down the doors and break in, overwhelming the guards.
Eustace and his host went out again, and presently
reported that the Marshal de Meilleraye had been half

killed, but had been rescued by the Coadjutor, who was giving the people all manner of promises. This was verified by shouts of " Vive le Roi!" And by and by the crowd came past once more, surrounding the carriage, on the top of which was seated the Coadjutor, in his violet robes, but with his skull cap away, and his cheek bleeding from the blow of a stone. He was haranguing, gesticulating, blessing, doing all in his power to pacify the crowd, and with the hope of the release of the councillors all was quieting down; and Clément, after reconnoitring, thought it safe to order the carriage to take home his guests.

"No one can describe," said my sister, " how good and sweet Madame was, though she looked so like a Puritan dame. Her face was so wonderfully calm and noble, like some grand old saint in a picture; and it lighted up so whenever her son came near her, I wanted to ask her blessing! And I think she gave it inwardly. She curtsied, and would have kissed my hand, as being only bourgeois, while I was noble; but I told her I would have no such folly, and I made her give me a good motherly embrace!"

"I hope she gave you something to eat," I said, laughing.

"Oh yes; we had an excellent meal. She made us eat before sending us home, soup, and *ragoût*, and chocolate—excellent chocolate. She had it brought as

soon as possible, because Eustace looked so pale and
tired.   Oh, Meg! she is the very best creature I have
seen in France.   Your Rambouillets are nothing to her!
I hope I may see her often again!"

And while Eustace marvelled if this were a passing
tumult or the beginning of a civil war, my most immediate wonder was what my mother would say to this
adventure.

CHAPTER XVI.

THE BARRICADES.

My mother did not come home till the evening, when the streets had become tolerably quiet. She had a strange account to give, for she had been at the palace all the time in attendance on Queen Henrietta, who tried in vain to impress her sister-in-law with a sense that the matter was serious. Queen Anne of Austria was too proud to believe that a parliament and a mob could do any damage to the throne of France, whatever they might effect in England.

There she sat in her grand cabinet, and with her were the Cardinal, the Duke of Longueville, and many other gentlemen, especially Messieurs de Nogent and de Beautru, who were the wits, if not the buffoons of the Court, and who turned all the reports they heard into ridicule. The Queen-Regent smiled in her haughty way, but the Queen of England laid her hand sadly on my mother's arm and said, " Alas, my dear friend, was it not thus that once we laughed ? "

Presently in came Marshal de la Meilleraye and the Coadjutor, and their faces and gestures showed plainly that they were seriously alarmed; but M. de Beautru, nothing daunted, turned to the Regent, saying, "How ill Her Majesty must be, since *M. le Coadjuteur* is come to bring her extreme unction," whereupon there was another great burst of applause and laughter.

The Coadjutor pretended not to hear, and addressing the Queen told her that he had come to offer his services to her at a moment of pressing danger. Anne of Austria only vouchsafed a little nod with her head, by way at once of thanks, and showing how officious and super-fluous she thought him, while Nogent and Beautru con-tinued to mimic the dismay of poor Broussel, seized in his dressing-gown and slippers, and the shrieks of his old housekeeper from the window.

"Did no one silence them for being so unmanly?" cried Annora, as she heard this.

"Child, thou art foolish!" said my mother with dignity. "Why should the resistance of *canaille* like that be observed at all, save to make sport?"

For my poor mother, since she had been dipped again into the Court atmosphere, had learned to look on whatever was not noble, as not of the same nature with herself. However, she said that Marshal de la Meilleraye, a thorough soldier, broke in by assuring the Queen that the populace were in arms, howling for Broussel, and the

Coadjutor began to describe the fierce tumult through which he had made his way, but the Cardinal only gave his dainty provoking Italian smile, and the Queen-Regent proudly affirmed that there neither was nor could be a revolt.

"We know," added Mazarin, in his blandest tone of irony, " that M. le Coadjuteur is so devoted to the Court, and so solicitous for his flock, that a little over-anxiety must be pardoned to him ! "

This was while shouts of " *Broussel ! Broussel !* " were echoing through the palace, and in a few moments came the Lieutenant-Colonel of the Guards to say that the populace were threatening to overpower the soldiers at the gates; and next came the Chancellor, nearly frightened out of his wits, saying that he had seen the people howling like a pack of wolves, carrying all sorts of strange weapons, and ready to force their way in. Then old Monsieur Guitauet, the Colonel of the Guards, declared " that the old rogue Broussel must be surrendered, dead or alive."

" The former step would not be accordant with the Queen's piety nor her justice," broke in the Coadjutor ; " the second might stop the tumult."

" I understand you, *Monsieur le Coadjuteur*," broke out the Queen. " You want me to set Broussel at liberty. I would rather strangle him with my own hands, and those who——"

And she held those plump white hands of hers almost close to the Archbishop's face, as if she were ready to do it, but Cardinal Mazarin whispered something in her ear which made her less violent, and the next moment the lieutenant of police came in, with such a terrific account of the fury of the mob and their numbers, that there was no more incredulity; it was plain that there was really a most frightful uproar, and both the Regent and the Cardinal entreated the Coadjutor to go down and pacify the people by promises. He tried to obtain from the Queen some written promise.

"He was right," said Eustace.

"Right!" cried my mother. "What! to seek to bind Her Majesty down by written words, like a base mechanical *bourgeois?* I am ashamed of you, my son! No, indeed, we all cried out upon him, Archbishop though he were, and told him that Her Majesty's word was worth ten thousand bonds."

"May it be so proved!" muttered Eustace, while my mother went on to describe how the Coadjutor was pressed, pushed, and almost dragged down the great staircase to speak to the infuriated people who were yelling and shrieking outside the court. Monsieur de Meilleraye went before him, backed by all the light horse drawn up in the court, and mounting his horse, drew his sword crying, " *Vive le Roi!* Liberty for Broussel!" He was met by a cry of "To arms, to arms!" and there was a rush against him, some trying to pull him off his horse, and one attacking him with a rusty old sword. The Marshal fired at him and he fell, severely wounded, just as the Coadjutor came down, and seeing him lying in the gutter like one dead, knelt down by him, heard his confession, and absolved him.

(It was afterwards said that the man was a picklock, but we always suspected that the Coadjutor had made the worst of him by way of enhancing a good story.)

Just as the absolution was finished, some more of the mob came up, and one threw a stone which hit the Archbishop on the cheek, and another pointed a musket at him. " Unhappy man," he cried, " if your father saw you ! " This seemed to touch the man ; he cried : " *Vive le Coadjuteur !* " And so easily were the people swayed, that they all began to applaud him to the skies, and he led them off to the market-place.

" We thought ourselves rid of them," said my mother, " we began to breathe again, and I was coming home, but, bah ! no such thing ! They are all coming back, thirty or forty thousand of them, only without their weapons. At least the gentlemen said so, but I am sure they had them hidden. Up comes *M. le Coadjuteur* again, the Marshal de Meilleraye leading him by the hand up to the Queen, and saying : ' Here, Madame, is one to whom I owe my life, but to whom your Majesty owes the safety of the State, nay, perhaps of the palace.' "

The Queen smiled, seeing through it all, said my mother, and the Coadjutor broke in : " The matter is not myself, Madame, it is Paris, now disarmed and submissive, at your Majesty's feet."

" It is very guilty, and far from submissive," said the Queen angrily ; " pray, if it were so furious, how can it have been so rapidly tamed ? "   And then M. de Meilleraye must needs break in furiously : " Madame, an honest man cannot dissemble the state of things.   If Broussel is not set at liberty, to-morrow there will not be one stone upon another at Paris."

But the Queen was firm, and put them both down, only saying : " Go and rest, Monsieur, you have worked hard."

" Was that all the thanks he had ? " exclaimed Annora.

" Of course it was, child.   The Queen and the Cardinal knew very well that the tumult was his work ; or at least immensely exaggerated by him, just to terrify her into releasing that factious old mischief-maker ! Why, he went off I know not where, haranguing them from the top of his carriage ! "

" Ah ! that was where we saw him," said Nan. " Madame, indeed there was nothing exaggerated in the tumult.   It was frightful.   They made ten times the

noise our honest folk do in England, and did ten times
less. If they had been English, M. Broussel would be
safe at home now!"

"No, the tumult was not over-painted, that I can
testify," said my brother.

But when my mother came to hear how he and
Annora had witnessed the scene from the windows of M.
Darpent's house, her indignation knew no bounds. I
never saw her so angry with Eustace as she now was,
that he should have taken his sister into the house of one
of these councillors; a *bourgeois* house was bad enough,
but that it should have been actually one of the disaffected, and that the Darpent carriage should have been
seen at our door, filled her with horror. It was enough
to ruin us all for ever with the Court.

"What have we to do with the Court?" cried my
sister, and this, of course, only added fuel to the flame,
till at last my mother came to declaring that she should
never trust her daughter with my brother again, for he
was not fit to take care of her.

But we were all surprised by Eustace, when he bade
my mother good-night, quietly bending his dark curled
head, and saying: "My mother, I ask your pardon, I am
sorry I offended you."

"My son, my dear son!" she cried, embracing him.
"Never think of it more, only if we never go home, I
cannot have your sister made a mere *bourgeoise.*"

"How could you, brother!" cried Annora, waiting outside the door. "Now you have owned yourself in the wrong!"

"I have not said so, Nan," he answered. "I have simply said I was sorry to have offended my mother, and that is true; I could not sleep under her displeasure."

"But you do not care about ruining yourself with this perfidious foreign Court."

"Not a rush, so long as I do not bring Meg and her son into danger."

Things were quiet that night, but every one knew that it was only a lull in the storm.

I set off to morning mass with my son and little Armantine as usual, thinking all would be quiet so early in our part of the city, but before the service was over there was the dull roar of the populace in a fury to be heard in the distance, and Nicole met me at the church door entreating me to get home as quickly as possible.

To my dismay there was a large heavy chain across the end of the street, not such as to stop foot passengers, but barring the way against carriages, and the street was fast filling with shopkeepers, apprentices, market-women, and all sorts of people. The children clung to my hands, half frightened and half eager. Suddenly we saw a carriage stopped by the chain, and the people crowding round it. Out of it sprang two gentlemen and a lady, and began hurrying forward like people hunted. I drew

the children back into the church porch, and was shocked
to see that those who were then fleeing in haste and
terror were the Chancellor, M. Séguier, with his brother,
the Bishop of Meaux, and his daughter the beautiful
young Duchess de Sully.   I tried to attract their attention and draw them into the church as a place of safety,
but they were in too much haste and terror to perceive
me, and a man began shouting after them :

"To arms, friends, to arms !   There's the enemy.   Kill
him ! and we shall have vengeance for all we suffer !"

The mob rushed after, shouting horribly.   Armantine
began to cry, and I took her in my arms, while Nicole
held my son.

The whole crowd rushed past us, never heeding us,
as we stood above them, and as we were only thirty
yards from home I hoped soon to reach it, though I
hesitated, as the screeches, yells, and howls were still to
be heard lower down the street, and fresh parties of men,
women, and children kept rushing down to join the
throng.   If it should surge back again before we could
get home, what would become of us ?

Suddenly Gaspard cried out : "My uncle !"   And
there was indeed my brother.   "Good heavens !" he
cried, "you there, sister !   They told me you were gone
to church, but I could hardly believe it !   Come home
before the mob comes back."

I asked anxiously for the Chancellor, and heard he

had escaped into the Hôtel de Luynes, which was three doors beyond ours. He had set out át six in the morning for the palace, it was believed to take orders for breaking up the Parliament. His daughter, thinking there might be danger, chose to go with him, and so did his brother the Bishop; but the instant he was known to be entangled in the streets, the mob rose on him, the chains were put up, he had to leave his carriage and flee on foot to the Hôtel de Luynes, where his brother-in-law lived. There the door was open, but no one was up but an old servant, and, in the utmost terror, the unhappy Chancellor rushed into a little wainscoted closet, where he shut himself up, confessing his sins to the Bishop, believing his last moments were come. In fact, the mob did search all over the hotel, some meaning to make him a hostage for Broussel, and others shouting that they would cut him to pieces to show what fate awaited the instruments of tyranny. They did actually beat against the wainscot of his secret chamber, but hearing nothing, they left the spot, but continued to keep guard round the house, shouting out execrations against him.

Meantime Eustace had brought us safely home, where the first thing we did was to hurry up to the balcony, where Annora was already watching anxiously.

Presently, Marshal de Meilleraye and his light horse came galloping and clattering down the street, while the mob fled headlong, hither and thither, before them. A

carriage was brought out, and the Chancellor with his
brother and daughter was put into it, but as they were
driving off the mob rallied again and began to pursue
them. A shot was fired, and a poor woman, under a
heavy basket, fell. There was another outburst of curses,
screams, howls, yells, shots; and carriage, guards, people,
all rushed past us, the coach going at the full speed of
its six horses, amid a shower of stones, and even bullets,
the guards galloping after, sometimes firing or cutting
with their swords, the people keeping up with them at a
headlong pace, pelting them with stones and dirt, and
often firing at them, for, indeed, the poor young Duchess
received a wound before they could reach the palace.
Meanwhile others of the mob began ransacking the
Hôtel de Luynes in their rage at the Chancellor's escape,
and they made dreadful havoc of the furniture, although
they did not pillage it.

My mother wept bitterly, declaring that the evil days
she had seen in England were pursuing her to France ;
and we could not persuade her that we were in no danger,
until the populace, having done their worst at the Hôtel
de Luynes, drifted away from our street. Eustace could
not of course bear to stay shut up and knowing nothing,
and he and the Abbé both went out different ways, leaving
us to devour our anxiety as best we could, knowing nothing
but that there was a chain across each end of our street,
with a double row of stakes on either side, banked up

with earth, stones, straw, all sorts of things, and guarded
by men with all manner of queer old weapons that had
come down from the wars of the League. Eustace even
came upon one of the old-fashioned arquebuses standing
on three legs to be fired; and, what was worse, there was
a gorget with the portrait of the murderer of Henri III.
enamelled on it, and the inscription " S. Jacques Clément,"
but the Coadjutor had the horrible thing broken up
publicly. My brother said things did indeed remind
him of the rusty old weapons that were taken down at
the beginning of the Rebellion. He had been to M. Darpent's, and found him exceedingly busy, and had learned
from him that the Coadjutor was at the bottom of all this
day's disturbance. Yes, Archbishop de Gondi himself.
He had been bitterly offended at the mocking, mistrustful
way in which his services had been treated, and besides,
reports came to him that the Cardinal talked of sending
him to Quimper Corentin, and Broussel to Havre, and
the Chancellor to dismiss the Parliament ! He had taken
counsel with his friends, and determined to put himself
at the head of the popular movement and be revenged
upon the Court, and one of his familiar associates, M.
d'Argenteuil, had disguised himself as a mason, and led
the attack with a rule in his hand, while a lady, Madame
Martineau, had beaten the drum and collected the throng
to guard the gates and attack the Chancellor. There
were, it was computed, no less than 1260 barricades all

over Paris, and the Parliament was perfectly amazed at the excitement produced by the capture of Broussel. Finding that they had such supporters, the Parliament was more than ever determined to make a stand for its rights—whatever they might be.

The Queen had sent to command the Coadjutor to appease the sedition, but he had answered that he had made himself so odious by his exertions of the previous day that he could not undertake what was desired of him.

The next thing we heard was that the First President, Mathieu Molé, one of the very best men then living, had gone at the head of sixty-six Counsellors of Parliament, two and two, to seek an audience of the Queen. They were followed by a huge multitude, who supposed Broussel to be still at the Palais Royal.

The Counsellors were admitted, but the Queen was as obdurate as ever. She told them that they, their wives and children, should answer for this day's work, and that a hundred thousand armed men should not force her to give up her will. Then she got up from her chair, went out of the room, and slammed the door! It is even said that she talked of hanging a few of the Counsellors from the windows to intimidate the mob; but Mademoiselle assured me that this was not true; though M. de Meilleraye actually proposed cutting off Broussel's head and throwing it out into the street.

The Counsellors were kept waiting two hours in the

Great Gallery, while the mob roared outside, and the
Cardinal, the Dukes of Orleans and Longueville, and
other great nobles, argued the matter with the Queen.
The Cardinal was, it seems, in a terrible fright. The
Queen, full of Spanish pride and high courage, would
really have rather perished than yielded to the populace ;
but Mazarin was more and more terrified, and at last she
yielded, and consented to his going to the Counsellors to
promise the release of the prisoners. He was trembling
all over, and made quite an absurd appearance, and presently the Parliament men appeared again, carrying huge
sealed letters ; Broussel's was borne by his nephew in
triumph. We could hear the *Vivats!* with which the
people greeted them, as the promise of restoration was
made known. At eleven at night there was a fresh outcry, but this was of joy, for M. Blancmesnil had actually
come back from Vincennes ; but the barricades were not
taken down. There was to be no laying down of arms
till Broussel appeared, and there were strange noises all
night, preventing sleep.

At eight o'clock the next morning Broussel had not
appeared ; the people were walking about in a sullen
rage, and this was made worse by a report that there
were 10,000 soldiers in the Bois de Boulogne ready to
chastise the people. We could see from our house-top
the glancing of arms at every barricade where the sun
could penetrate, and in the midst came one of the servants
announcing Monsieur Clément Darpent.

He had a sword by his side, and pistols at his belt, and he said that he was come to assure the ladies that there would be no danger for them. If any one tried to meddle with the house, we might say we were friends of M. Darpent, and we should be secure. If the account of the soldiers outside were true, the people were determined not to yield to such perfidy; but he did not greatly credit it, only it was well to be prepared.

"Alas! my friend," said Eustace, "this has all too much the air of rebellion."

"We stand on our rights and privileges," said Darpent. "We uphold them in the King's name against the treachery of a Spanish woman and an Italian priest."

"You have been sorely tried," said Eustace; "but I doubt me whether anything justifies taking arms against the Crown."

· "Ah! I am talking to a Cavalier," said Clément. "But I must not argue the point. I must to my barricade."

Nan here came forward, and desired him to carry her commendations and thanks to *Madame sa mère*, and he bowed, evidently much gratified. She durst not go the length of offering her good wishes, and she told me I ought to have been thankful to her for the forbearance, when, under a strong sense of duty, I reproved her. Technically he was only Maître Darpent, and his mother only would have been called Mademoiselle. Monsieur

and Madame were much more jealously limited to nobility
than they are now becoming, and the Darpents would not
purchase a patent of nobility to shelter themselves from
taxation.   For, as Eustace said, the *bourgeoisie* had its
own chivalry of ideas.

There was no more fighting.   By ten o'clock Broussel
was in the city, the chains were torn down, the barricades
levelled, and he made a triumphal progress.   He was
taken first to Notre Dame, and as he left the carriage his
old dressing-gown was almost torn to pieces, every one
crowding to kiss it, or his feet, calling him their father
and protector, and anxiously inquiring for his health.   A
Te Deum was sung—if not so splendid, much more full
of the ring of joy than the grand one two days before !
Engravings of his portrait were sold about the streets,
bearing the inscription " Pierre Broussel, father of his
country ;" and the good-natured old man seemed quite
bewildered at the honours that had befallen him.

There were a few more alarms that night and the
next day, but at last they subsided, the barricades were
taken down, and things returned to their usual state, at
least to all outward appearance.

CHAPTER XVII.

A PATIENT GRISEL.

MATTERS seemed to be getting worse all round us both in France and England. King Charles was in the hands of his enemies, and all the good news that we could hear from England was that the Duke of York had escaped in a girl's dress, and was on board the fleet at Helvoetsluys, where his brother the Prince of Wales joined him.

And my own dear brother, Lord Walwyn, declared that he could no longer remain inactive at Paris, so far from intelligence, but that he must be with the Princes, ready to assist in case anything should be attempted on the King's behalf. We much dreaded the effect of the Dutch climate on his health. And while tumultuous assemblies were constantly taking place in Parliament, and no one could guess what was coming next, we did not like parting with our protector; but he said that he was an alien, and could do nothing for us. The army was on its way home, and with it our brother de Solivet, and M. d'Aubépine; and his clear duty was to be ready to engage in the cause of his own King. We were in no danger at Paris, our sex was sufficient protection, and if we were really alarmed, there could be no reason against our fleeing to Nid de Merle. Nay, perhaps, if the Court were made to take home the lesson, we might be allowed to reside there, and be unmolested in making improvements. He had another motive, which he only whispered to me.

" I cannot, and will not, give up my friend Darpent; and it is not fitting to live in continual resistance to my mother. It does much harm to Annora, who is by no means inclined to submit, and if I am gone there can be no further question of intercourse."

I thought this was hard upon us all. Had we not met M. Darpent at the Hôtel Rambouillet, and was he not a fit companion for us ?

" Most assuredly," said Eustace ; " but certain sentiments may arise from companionship which in her case were better avoided."

As you may imagine, my grandchildren, I cried out in horror at the idea that if M. Darpent were capable of such presumption, my sister, a descendant of the Ribaumonts, could stoop for a moment to favour a mere *bourgeois;* but Eustace, Englishman as he was, laughed at my indignation, and said Annora was more of the Ribmont than the de Ribaumont, and that he would not be accessory either to the breaking of hearts or to letting her become rebellious, and so that he should put temptation out of her way. I knew far too well what was becoming to allow myself to suppose for a moment that Eustace thought an inclination between the two already could exist. I forgot how things had been broken up in England.

As to Annora, she thought Eustace's right place was with the Princes, and she would not stretch out a finger to hold him back, only she longed earnestly that he would take us with him. Could he not persuade our mother that France was becoming dangerous, and that she would be safe in Holland ? But of course he only laughed at that; and we all saw that unless the Queen of England chose to follow her sons, there was no chance of my mother leaving the Court.

" No, my sister," said Eustace tenderly, " there is nothing for you to do but to endure patiently. It is very hard for you to be both firm and resolute, and at the same time dutiful; but it is a noble part in its very difficulty, and my Nan will seek strength for it."

Then the girl pressed up to him, and told him that one thing he must promise her, namely, that he would prevent my mother from disposing of her hand without his consent.

" As long as you are here I am safe," said she ; " but when you are gone I do not know what she may attempt. And here is this Solivet son of hers coming too ! "

"Solivet has no power over you," said Eustace.
"You may make yourself easy, Nan. Nobody can marry
you without my consent, for my father made me your
guardian. And I doubt me if your portion, so long as I
am living, be such as to tempt any man to wed such a
little fury, even were we at home."

"Thanks for the hint, brother," said Annora. "I
will take care that any such suitor *shall* think me a
fury."

"Nay, child, in moderation! Violence is not strength.
Nay, rather it exhausts the forces. Resolution and submission are our watchwords."

How noble he looked as he said it, and how sad it
was to part with him! My mother wept most bitterly,
and said it was cruel to leave us to our fate, and that he
would kill himself in the Dutch marshes; but when the
actual pain of parting with him was over, I am not sure
that she had not more hope of carrying out her wishes. She
would have begun by forbidding Annora to go, attended
only by the servants, to prayers at the English ambassador's: but Eustace had foreseen this, and made arrange-
ments with a good old knight and his lady, Sir Francis
Ommaney, always to call for my sister on their way to
church, and she was always ready for them. My mother
used to say that her devotion was all perverseness, and
now and then, when more than usually provoked with
her, would declare that it was quite plain that her poor

child's religion was only a heresy, since it did not make her a better daughter.

That used to sting Annora beyond all measure. Sometimes she would reply by pouring out a catalogue of all the worst offences of our own Church, and Heaven knows she could find enough of them! Or at others she would appeal to the lives of all the best people she had ever heard of in England, and especially of Eustace, declaring that she knew she herself was far from good, but that was not the fault of her religion, but of herself; and she would really strive to be submissive and obliging for many days afterwards.

Meantime the Prince of Condé had returned, and had met the Court at Ruel. M. d'Aubépine and M. de Solivet both were coming with him, and my poor little Cécile wrote letter after letter to her husband, quite correct in grammar and orthography, asking whether she should have the Hôtel d'Aubépine prepared, and hire servants to receive him ; but she never received a line in reply. She was very anxious to know whether the *concierge* had received any orders, and yet she could not bear to betray her ignorance.

I had been startled by passing in the street a face which I was almost sure belonged to poor Cécile's former enemy, Mademoiselle Gringrimeau, now the wife of Croquelebois, the *intendant* of the estate ; and setting old Nicole to work, I ascertained that this same agent and

his wife were actually at the Hôtel d'Aubépine, having
come to meet their master, but that no apartments were
made ready for him, as it was understood that being on
the staff he would be lodged in the Hôtel de Condé.

"His duty!" said Cécile; "he must fulfil his duty,
but at least I shall see him."

But to hear of the *intendant* and his wife made me
very uneasy.

The happier wives were going out in their carriages
to meet their husbands on the road, but Cécile did not
even know when he was coming, nor by what road.

"So much the better," said our English Nan. "If I
had a husband, I would never make him look foolish in
the middle of the road with a woman and a pack of
children hanging on him!"

No one save myself understood her English bashfulness, shrinking from all display of sentiment, and I—ah!
I had known such blissful meetings, when my Philippe
had been full of joy to see me come out to meet him.
Ah! will he meet me thus at the gates of Paradise? It
cannot be far off now!

I knew I should weep all the way if I set out with
my mother to meet her son; and Cécile was afraid both
of the disappointment if she did not meet her husband,
and of his being displeased if he should come. So she
only took with her Annora and M. de Solivet's two daughters,
Gabrielle and Petronille, who were fetched from the Con-

vent of the Visitation. There they sat in the carriage,
Nan told me, exactly alike in their *pensionnaire's* uniform,
stiff and shy on the edge of the seat, not daring to look
to the right or left, and answering under their breath, so
that she longed to shake them. I found afterwards that
the heretic Mademoiselle de Ribaumont was a fearful
spectacle to them, and that they were expecting her all
the time to break out in the praises of Luther, or of
Henry VIII., or of some one whom they had been taught
to execrate; and whenever she opened her lips they
thought she was going to pervert them, and were quite
surprised when she only made a remark, like other people,
on the carriages and horsemen who passed them.

Meanwhile Cécile saw her little girl and boy dressed
in their best, and again rehearsed the curtsey and the
bow and the little speeches with which they were to
meet their father. She was sure, she said, that whatever
he might think of her, he must be enchanted with them;
and truly they had beautiful eyes, and Armantine was a
charming child, though Maurice was small and pale, and
neither equalled my Gaspard, who might have been a
White Ribaumont for height and complexion, resembling
much his uncle Walwyn, and yet in countenance like
his father. Then Cécile and I, long before it was reasonable, took our station near a window overlooking the
porte-cochère. I sat with my work, while the children
watched on the window-seat, and she, at every exclama-

tion of theirs, leaped up to look out, but only to see
some woodcutter with his pile of faggots, or a washer-
woman carrying home a dress displayed on its pole, or
an ell of bread coming in from the baker's; and she
resumed her interrupted conversation on her security
that for the children's sake her husband would set up
his household together with her at the Hôtel d'Aubépine.
She had been learning all she could, while she was with
us, and if she could only be such that he need not be
ashamed of her, and would love her only a little for his
children's sake, how happy she should be!

I encouraged her, for her little dull provincial convent air was quite gone; she had acquired the air of
society, my mother had taught her something of the art
of dress, and though nothing would ever make her
beautiful in feature, or striking in figure, she had such
a sweet, pleading, lovely expression of countenance that
I could not think how any one could resist her. At
last it was no longer a false alarm. The children cried
out, not in vain. The six horses were clattering under
the gateway, the carriage came in sight before the steps.
Cécile dropped back in her chair as pale as death, murmuring : " Tell me if he is there ! "

Alas ! " he " was not there. I only saw M. de
Solivet descend from the carriage and hand out my
mother, my sister, and his two daughters. I could but
embrace my poor sister-in-law, and assure her that I

would bring her tidings of her husband, and then hurry away with Gaspard that I might meet my half-brother at the *salon* door. There he was, looking very happy, with a daughter in each hand, and they had lighted up into something like animation, which made Petronille especially show that she might some day be pretty. He embraced me, like the good-natured friendly brother he had always been, and expressed himself perfectly amazed at the growth and beauty of my little Marquis, as well he might be, for my mother and I both agreed that there was not such another child among all the King's pages.

I asked, as soon as I could, for M. d'Aubépine, and heard that he was attending the Prince, who would, of course, first have to dress, and then to present himself to the Queen-Regent, and kiss her hand, after which he would go to Madame de Longueville's reception of the King. It was almost a relief to hear that the Count was thus employed, and I sent my son to tell his aunt that she might be no longer in suspense.

I asked Solivet whether we might expect the young man on leaving the Louvre, and he only shrugged his shoulders and said: "What know I?" It became plain to me that he would not discuss the matter before his daughters, now fourteen and fifteen, and we all had to sit down to an early supper, after which they were to be taken back to their convent. Madame d'Aubépine appeared, and was quite cheerful, for she figured to herself once more that her husband was only detained by his duties and his value to his Prince, and was burning every moment to see his little ones. She asked questions about him, and became radiant when she heard of his courage at Lens, and the compliments that M. le Prince had paid to him.

After supper the little pensionnaires were to be taken back, and as some lady must escort them, I undertook the charge, finding with great delight that their father would accompany them likewise. I effaced myself as much as I could on the way, and let the father and daughters talk to one another; and they chattered freely about their tasks, and works, and playfellows, seeming very happy with him.

But on the way home was my opportunity, and I asked what my half-brother really thought of M. d'Aubépine.

"He is a fine young man," he said.

"You have told me that before; but what hopes are there for his wife?"

"Poor little thing," returned Solivet.

"Can he help loving her?" I said.

"Alas! my sister, he has been in a bad school, and has before him an example—of courage, it is true, but not precisely of conjugal affection."

"Is it true, then," I asked, "that the Princess of

Condé is kept utterly in the background in spite of her mother-in-law, and that the Prince publishes his dislike to her?"

"Perfectly true," said my brother. "When a hero, adored by his officers, actually declares that the only thing he does not wish to see in France is his wife, what can you expect of them? Even some who really love their wives bade them remain at home, and will steal away to see them with a certain shame; and for Aubé- pine, he is only too proud to resemble the Prince in being married against his will to a little half-deformed child, who is to be avoided."

I cried out at this, and demanded whether my little sister-in-law could possibly be thus described. He owned that she was incredibly improved, and begged my pardon and hers, saying that he was only repeating what Aubépine either believed or pretended to believe her to be.

"If I could only speak with him!" I said. "For my husband's sake I used to have some influence with him. I would give the world to meet him before he sees the *intendant* and his wife. Could we contrive it?"

In a few moments we had settled it. Happily we were both in full dress, in case friends should have dropped in on us. Both of us had the *entrée* at Madame de Longueville's, and it would be quite correct to pay her our compliments on the return of her brother.

I believe Solivet a little questioned whether one so

headstrong had not better be left to himself, but he
allowed that no one had ever done as much with Armand
d'Aubépine as my husband and myself, and when he
heard my urgent wish to forestal the *intendant*, whose
wife was Cécile's old tyrant, Mademoiselle de Gringrimeau, he thought it worth the venture. He said I was
a warlike Gildippe still, and that he would stand by me.

So the coachman received his orders; we fell in among
the long line of carriages, and in due time made our way
to the *salon*, where Madame la Duchesse de Longueville
sat enthroned in all the glory of her fair hair and
beautiful complexion, toying with her fan as she conversed with the Prince of Marsillac, the most favoured at
that time of a whole troop of admirers and devoted slaves.
She was not an intellectual woman herself, but she had
beyond all others whom I ever saw the power of leading
captive the very ablest men.

The hero had not yet come from the palace, and
having made our compliments, and received a gracious
smile and nod, we stood aside, waiting and conversing
with others, and in some anxiety lest the Prince should
be detained at the Louvre. However, before long he
came, and his keen eagle face, and the stars on his breast,
flashed on us, as he returned the greetings of one group
after another in his own peculiar manner, haughty, and
yet not without a certain charm.

A troop of officers followed, mingling with the gay

crowd of ladies and gentlemen, and among them Solivet
pointed out the Count d'Aubépine. I should not otherwise have known him, so much was he altered in these
six years, changing him from youth to manhood. His
hair was much darker, he had a small pointed beard, and
the childish contour of cheek and chin had passed away,
and he was altogether developed, but there was something that did not reassure me. He seemed to have lost,
with his boyhood, that individuality which we had once
loved, and to have passed into an ordinary officer, like
all the rest of the gay, dashing, handsome, but often
hardened-looking men, who were enjoying their triumphant
return into ladies' society.

Solivet had accosted him. I saw his eye glance
anxiously round, then he seemed reassured, and came
towards me with some eagerness, greeting me with some
compliment, I know not what, on my appearance; but I
cut this as short as I could by saying: "Know you,
Monsieur, why I am here? I am come to ask you to
bestow a little half-hour on one who is longing to see
you."

"Madame, I am desolated to refuse you, but, you see,
I am in attendance, and on duty; I am not the master!"

However, my brother observed that he would not be
required for at least two hours, and his movements would
be quite free until the party broke up. And after a little
importunity, I actually carried him off, holding up his

hands and declaring that he could not withstand Madame
de Bellaise, so as to cast over his concession an air of
gallantry without which I believe his vanity would never
have yielded.

However, I had my hopes; I would not blame him
when I had such an advantage over him as having him
shut up with me in my coach, for we left Solivet to make
his excuses, and as we told him, for a hostage, to come
back when I released my prisoner. I trusted more to the
effect of the sight of my sweet little Cécile than to any
exhortation in my power; indeed, I thought I had better
keep him in good humour by listening amiably to his
explanation of the great favour that he was doing me in
coming to see Madame, my mother, and how indispensable
he was to M. le Prince.

He must have known what I was carrying him to
see, but he did not choose to show that he did, and when
he gave me his arm and I took him into the pansy *salon*,
there sat my mother with my sister, two or three old
friends who had come to congratulate her, and to see
M. de Solivet, and Cécile, who had not been able to persuade herself to send her children to bed, though she
knew not of my audacious enterprise.

I saw that he did not know her in the least, as he
advanced to my mother, as the lady of the house, and in
one moment I recollected how my grandfather had fallen
in love with my grandmother without knowing she was

his wife. Cécile, crimson all over, with her children beside her, sprang forward, her heart telling her who he was. " Ah, Monsieur, embrace your son," she murmured. And little Armantine and Maurice, as they had been tutored, made their pretty reverences, and said, "Welcome, my papa."

He really was quite touched. There was something, too, in the surroundings which was sympathetic. He embraced them all, and evidently looked at his wife with amazement, sitting down at last beside her with his little boy upon his knee.

We drew to the farther end of the room that they might be unembarrassed. Annora was indignant that we did not leave them alone, but I thought he wanted a certain check upon him, and that it was good for him to be in the presence of persons who expected him to be delighted to see his wife and children.

I believe that that quarter of an hour was actual pain to Cécile from the very overflowing rush of felicity. To have her husband seated beside her, with his son upon his knee, had been the dream and prayer of her life for six years, and now that it was gratified the very intensity of her hopes and fears choked her, made her stammer and answer at random, when a woman without her depth of affection might have put out all kinds of arts to win and detain him.

After a time he put the child down, but still held his

hand, came up to the rest of the company and mingled with it. I could have wished they had been younger and more fashionable, instead of a poor old Scottish cavalier and his wife, my mother's old contemporary Madame de Délincourt, and a couple of officers waiting for Solivet. Annora was the only young brilliant creature there, and she had much too low an opinion of M. d'Aubépine to have a word to say to him, and continued to converse in English with old Sir Andrew Macniven about the campaigns of the Marquis of Montrose, both of them hurling out barbarous names that were enough to drive civilised ears out of the room.

Our unwilling guest behaved with tolerably good grace, and presently made his excuse to my mother and me, promising immediately to send back Solivet to his friends. His wife went with him into the outer room, and when in a few minutes Armantine ran back to call me—

"Papa is gone, and mamma is crying," she said.

It was true, but they were tears of joy. Cécile threw herself on my bosom perfectly overwhelmed with happiness, poor little thing! declaring that she owed it all to me, and that though he could not remain now, he had promised that she should hear from him. He was enchanted with his children; indeed, how could he help it? And she would have kept me up all night, discussing every hair of his moustache, every tone in the few words he had spoken to her. When at last I parted from her I could not help being very glad. Was the victory indeed won, and would my Philippe's sister become a happy wife?

I trusted that now he had seen her he would be armed against Madame Croquelebois, who you will remember had been his grandmother's *dame de compagnie*, and a sort of governess to him. She had petted him as much as she had afterwards tyrannised over his poor little wife, and might still retain much influence over him, which she was sure to exert against me. But at any rate he could not doubt of his wife's adoration for him.

We waited in hope. We heard of the Prince in attendance on the Queen-Regent, and we knew his *aide-de-camp* could not be spared, and we went on expecting all the morning and all the evening, assuring Cécile that military duty was inexorable, all the time that we were boiling over with indignation.

My mother was quite as angry as we were, and from her age and position could be more effective. She met M. d'Aubépine one evening at the Louvre, and took him to task, demanding when his wife was to hear from him, and fairly putting him out of countenance in the presence of the Queen of England. She came home triumphant at what she had done, and raised our hopes again, but in fact, though it impelled him to action, there was now mortified vanity added to indifference and impatience of the yoke.

There was a letter the next day.   Half an hour after receiving it I found Cécile sunk down on the floor of her apartment, upon which all her wardrobe was strewn about as if to be packed up.   She fell into my arms weeping passionately, and declaring she must leave us.   To leave us and set up her *ménage* with her husband had always been her ambition, so it was plain that this was not what she meant; but for a long time she neither would nor could tell me, or moan out anything but "a convent," "how could he ?" and "my children."

At last she let me read the letter, and a cruel one it was, beginning " Madame," and giving her the choice of returning to Château d'Aubépine under the supervision of Madame Croquelebois, or of entering a convent, and sending her son to be bred up at the Château under a tutor and the *intendant*.   She had quite long enough lived with Madame de Bellaise, and that young Englishman, her brother, who was said to be charming.

It was an absolute insult to us all, and as I saw at once was the work of Madame Croquelebois, accepted by the young Count as a convenient excuse for avoiding the *ennui* and expense of setting up a household with his wife, instead of living a gay bachelor life with his Prince. I did not even think it was his handwriting except the signature, an idea which gave the first ray of comfort to my poor sister-in-law.   It was quite provoking to find that she had no spirit to resent, or even to blame; she

only wept that any one should be so cruel, and, quite
hopeless of being heard in her own defence, was ready to
obey, and return under the power of her oppressor, if only
she might keep her son. All the four years she had
lived with us had not taught her self-assertion, and
the more cruelly she was wounded, the meeker she
became.

The Abbé said she was earning a blessing; but I felt,
like Annora, much inclined to beat her, when she would
persist in loving and admiring that miserable fellow
through all, and calling him "so noble.".

We did not take things by any means so quietly.
We were the less sorry for my brother's absence that such
an insinuation almost demanded a challenge, though in
truth I doubt whether they would have dared to make it
had he been at hand. Annora did wish she could take
sword or pistols in hand and make him choke on his own
words, and she was very angry that our brother de Solivet
was much too cool and prudent to take Eustace's quarrel
on himself.

Here, however, it was my mother who was most
reasonable, and knew best how to act. She said that it
was true that as this was my house, and the charge of
Madame d'Aubépine had been committed to me, I had
every right to be offended; but as she was the eldest lady
in the house it was suitable for her to act. She wrote a
billet to him demanding a personal interview with him,

that he might explain the insinuations which concerned the honour of herself, her son, and her daughter.

I believe a duel would have been much more agreeable to him than such a meeting, but my mother so contrived it that he knew that he could not fail to meet her without its being known to the whole Court, and that he could not venture. So he came, and I never saw anything more admirably managed than the conference was on my mother's part, for she chose to have me present as mistress of the house. She had put on her richest black velvet suit, and looked a most imposing *châtelaine*, and though he came in trying to carry it off with military bravado and nonchalance, he was evidently ill at ease.

My mother then demanded of him, in her own name, her son's, and mine, what right or cause he had to make such accusations, as he had implied, respecting our house.

He laughed uneasily, and tried to make light of it, talking of reports, and inferences, and so on; but my mother, well assured that there was no such scandal, drove him up into a corner, and made him confess that he had heard nothing but from Madame Croquelebois. My mother then insisted on that lady being called for, sending her own sedan chair to bring her.

Now the Baronne de Ribaumont Walwyn was a veritable *grande dame*, and Madame Croquelebois, in spite of her sharp nose and sharper tongue, was quite cowed by her, and absolutely driven to confess that she had not heard a word against Madame la Comtesse. All that she had gone upon was the fact of their residence in the same house, and that a servant of hers had heard from a servant of ours that M. le Baron gave her his hand to go in to dinner every day when there were no visitors.

It all became plain then. The *intendant's* wife, who had never forgiven me for taking her victim away from her, had suggested this hint as an excuse for withdrawing the Countess from me, without obliging the Count to keep house with her, and becoming the attentive husband, who seemed, to his perverted notions, a despicable being. Perhaps neither of them had expected the matter to be taken up so seriously, and an old country-bred Huguenot, as Madame Croquelebois had originally been, thought that as we were at Court, gallantry was our natural atmosphere.

Having brought them to confession, we divided them. My mother talked to the *intendante,* and made her perceive what a wicked, cruel injustice and demoralisation she was leading her beloved young Count into committing, injuring himself and his children, till the woman actually wept, and allowed that she had not thought of it ; she wanted to gratify him, and she felt it hard and ungrateful that she should not watch over his wife and children as his grandmother had always intended.

On my side I had M. d'Aubépine, and at last I

worked down to the Armand I had known at Nancy, not indeed the best of subjects, but still infinitely better than the conceited, reckless man who had appeared at first. The one thing that touched him was that I should think him disrespectful to me, and false to his friendship for my husband. He really had never thought his words would hurt me for a moment. He actually shed tears at the thought of my Philippe, and declared that nothing was farther from his intention than any imputation on any one belonging to me.

But bah! he was absolutely driven to find some excuse! How could he play the devoted husband to a little ugly imbecile like that, who would make him ridiculous every moment they appeared together? Yes, he knew I had done the best I could for her, but what was she after all? And her affection was worst of all. Everybody would make game of him.

There was no getting farther. The example of the Prince of Condé and the fear of ridicule had absolutely steeled his heart and blinded his eyes. He could not and would not endure the innocent wife who adored him.

Finally, my mother, calling in Solivet, came to the following arrangement, since it was plain that we must part with our inmates. Cécile and her children were to be installed in the Hôtel d'Aubépine, to which her husband did not object, since he would be either in attendance on the Prince, or with his regiment. This was better than sending her either to a convent or to the country, since she would still be within our reach, although to our great vexation we could not prevail so far as to hinder Madame Croquelebois from being installed as her duenna, the *intendant* himself returning to La Vendée.

To our surprise, Cécile did not seem so much dismayed at returning under the power of her tyrant as we had expected. It was doing what her husband wished, and living where she would have news of him, and perhaps sometimes see him.

That was all she seemed to think about, except that she would have her children still with her, and not be quite cut off from us.

And I took this consolation, that she was in better health, and a woman of twenty-two could not be so easily oppressed as a sickly child of sixteen.

But we were very unhappy about it, and Annora almost frantic, above all at Cécile's meek submission. She was sure the poor thing would be dead in a month, and then we should be sorry.

CHAPTER XVIII.

My mother declared that Madame d'Aubépine would fare the better if we left her alone and did not excite the jealousy of Madame Croquelebois, who would be quite capable of carrying her off into the country if she were interfered with.

Indeed it was not an easy or a pleasant thing to go about Paris just then, and we were obliged to stay at home. The town was in a restless state, mobs went about, hooting or singing political songs, or assembled in front of the Louvre to abuse the Cardinal, and any one who was supposed to belong to the Court party might at any time be mobbed. Annora and I much missed the explanations that our brother, Lord Walwyn, used to make to us; and the listening to his conversations with M. Darpent. The Duchess de Rambouillet and her family had wisely retired to their estates, so that there were no more meetings in the Salon Bleu; and after what my brother had said to me, I durst not make the slightest

demonstration towards Clément Darpent, though I continued to give my weekly receptions to our poor hungry
cavaliers, as I had promised Eustace that I would do.
It was from one of them, Sir Andrew Macniven, a clever
man who had been a law student in Scotland and at
Leyden, that we came to some understanding of what
was going on around us.

Under the great Cardinal de Richelieu, the Crown had
taken more authority than ever, and raised taxes at its
will. The Parliament was only permitted to register
the edicts of the Crown, but not to refuse them, as it
claimed to do. As nobody who was noble paid taxes,
the *noblesse* did not care, and there had hitherto seemed
to be no redress. But at this moment, when the war
taxes were weighing more heavily than ever, and the
demand of a house-tax had irritated the people of Paris,
there were a very large number of the nobility much
incensed against Cardinal Mazarin, and very jealous of
his favour with the Queen-Regent. What they would
endure from a French nobleman like Richelieu they
abhorred from a low-born foreigner such as Mazarin was ;
and it seemed to the Parliament that this was the
moment to make a stand, since they had the populace
on their side, and likewise so many of the Court party.
There was the Archbishop of Corinth, the Coadjutor to
the Archbishop of Paris, who had been mortally offended
by the way in which the Queen had treated him on

the day of the barricades; there was the handsome, fair-haired Duke of Beaufort, a grandson of Henri IV., who used to be called "*Le roi des halles*," he was such a favourite with the market-women; there was the clever brilliant Prince de Marsillac (you know well his Maxims, written after he had become Duke of Rochefoucauld). He could do anything with Madame de Longueville; and she was thought able to do anything with her brothers, the Princes of Condé and Conti.   Every one had been watching to see what side the Prince would take, but at this time he seemed inclined to the Crown, though it was not likely he could go on long without quarrelling with Mazarin.   All this made the Frondeurs hope much from beginning to resist; but I remember Sir Andrew said that he did not think that much would be done, for he did not believe that these nobles and princes cared in the least for relieving the people, but merely for overthrowing the Cardinal, and he could not find out that the Parliament had any definite scheme, or knew what they wished.   In fact, Sir Andrew dreaded any movement. He had been so much disappointed, and so broken-hearted at the loss of friends and the ruin of the country, that his only thought was to leave all alone.   And above all he so thought, when every letter from England told how the enemy were proceeding to hunt down his Sacred Majesty.

What a change it was when my son and I had to

go into waiting at the Louvre! Before the Queen-Regent there was nothing but vituperation of the Parliament, but the Duke of Orleans hated the Cardinal quite as much as the Parisians did ; and his daughter, Mademoiselle, wanted him to lead the Frondeurs, which he had not courage to do. She thought me a Frondeuse, and chatted to me of her plan of leading the party, together with the Prince of Condé, whom she eagerly desired to marry if his poor wife could be divorced. I used to shake my head at her and say I knew she was too good at the bottom to desire anything so shocking, and she took it in good part. She was much better than she chose to seem.

Thus the eve of the Epiphany came, and there was a feast for the King and his little companions. Gaspard had the Bean, and the Queen crowned him and made him King of the night. King Louis himself had to bend the knee, which he did with the best grace in the world. (You must all have seen the little enamelled Bean-flower badge that your father received on that night.)

Every one went to see the children at their feast, where the little English Lady Henrietta sat between her two royal cousins, looking like a rosebud, all ignorant, poor child, of the sad disaster which was falling on her. Her mother was looking on, smiling in the midst of her cares to see the children's glee.

The Queen-Regent was in the highest spirits. We had never seen her dignity so relax into merriment as when she set the little ones to dance together after the supper was over; but she sent them to bed early, much earlier than her sons desired. We heard his real Majesty saying to Gaspard, " M. le Marquis, since you are King of the Bean, command that we should be like all other revellers, and sit up till morning."

My boy looked up to me, and read in my face that he must not presume.

" Ah, sire !" said he, " though we are called kings, these ladies are the higher powers."

It was applauded as a grand witticism, although Gaspard meant it in all simplicity, and had no notion of the meaning attributed to it. Nay, he thought all the praise was approval of him as a good boy inducing the King to be obedient.

After the children had gone to bed, including Mademoiselle's three little half-sisters, dull little girls of whom she spoke contemptuously but always treated very kindly, she led the way to the apartment where her father was sitting by a great fire, fretful with gout, and wanting the amusement which she tried to give him by describing the children's diversions. Some one came and whispered something to her, and in the tone of one who has an excellent joke to rehearse she went up to the Duke of Orleans, exclaiming—

" Monsieur!   Here is news !   We are all to start for
St. Germain this very night !"

Monsieur made no answer, and immediately after
bade her good night.   She then went to her stepmother's
room, and I remained with some of the other ladies, who
were pretty well convinced that it was a true report, and
that the Queen had been only waiting the arrival of the
troops from the Low Countries to quit Paris and crush
the resistance of the Parliament.   What was to become
of us we did not know, whether we were to stay or go ;
but as we heard no more, and Mademoiselle came out
and went to bed, we followed her example.

Between three and four we were all awakened by a
loud knocking at the door, and Mademoiselle's shrill
voice calling out to her maids to open it.   Through the
anteroom, where the Comtesse de Fiesque and I were
sleeping, there came M. de Comminges.   Mademoiselle,
in her laced night-cap, rose on her pillows and asked—

" Are we going ?"

" Yes, Mademoiselle," was the reply.   " The King,
the Queen, and Monsieur, are waiting for you in the
court, and here is a letter from Monsieur."

She put it aside, saying she did not want Monsieur's
orders to make her obey those of the Queen, but he
begged her to read it.   She glanced at it, and then declared that she would be ready immediately.   M. de
Comminges departed, and then began the greatest bustle

imaginable, everybody dressing at once in the greatest
confusion, putting on each other's things by mistake,
and Mademoiselle talking—talking through all.

They were afraid to leave her behind, she said, lest
she should have headed a party.   No doubt M. le Prince
dreaded her influence, and so did the Queen.   They had
made her father issue his commands without warning
lest she should disobey.

In fact she had the greatest desire to disobey, only
she did not quite venture, and we her ladies had no
notion what we were to do, whether to stay or go, while
I was in great anxiety as to what they might have done
with my boy.

Somehow or other we all found ourselves in the court
of the Louvre, strongly lighted by flambeaux, and by the
windows of the building.   There stood a row of carriages ;
Mademoiselle called for hers, but it was not forthcoming,
and M. de Comminges, bowing low, offered her his own ;
but another gentleman came up and handed her into the
royal one, where already were the King and Queen, the
two Princesses of Condé, the Prince of Conti, and a lady.

I heard Mademoiselle asserting her right to one of
the best seats, and then declaring that she yielded " as
the young must give place to the old," a little cut at the
Princess Dowager of Condé.   She bade Madame de
Fiesque follow with her carriage and properties, and we
were left in the most wonderful confusion in that dark

court, the carriages moving away one after another, the
mounted servants carrying torches, and the guards tramp-
ling and clinking behind them; servants, gentlemen, and
ladies running about wildly, some of the women crying
and wringing their hands. Among these was Madame
de Fiesque, who was of a timid nature, and was frightened
out of her wits at the notion of having to follow, whither
she did not even know, while I was equally wild, though
I hope I did not make quite so much noise, about
my son.

One of the gentlemen at last came and spoke to us,
and told us that the King and Queen were gone to St.
Germain. It had all been determined upon for some
time past (as soon in fact as the Queen knew that the
Prince of Condé would support her, and that the troops
were near enough to be of use), and this night had been
chosen because she could get off more easily in a time of
revelry. Monsieur had known it all the evening, but
had been afraid to tell his daughter because of "her
ideas," which meant that he was by no means sure that
she might choose to obey, unless she were taken by surprise, but might want to represent the House of Orleans
at Paris. The Queen of England was not gone; and, as
to M. le Marquis de Nidemerle—

That question was answered by a sound of bare, patter-
ing feet, and a cry of "Mamma, mamma!" and my little
Marquis himself, with nothing on but his little white

shirt and black velvet breeches, his long hair streaming
behind him, came and threw himself on me, followed by
two or three more little fellows in the same state of
deshabille. "Oh, mamma!" he cried, "we thought they
were all gone, and had left us to be murdered by the
cruel Parliament; and then I saw you from the window
in the court." So there they all were, except one little
Count from Burgundy, who slept serenely through the
tumult.

By this time we could recollect that it was a January
night, and that we had better retreat into the great hall,
where the fire was not out. I had a great mind, since
we were thus deserted, to return home with my son, but
my poor Princess could not be left without a single
attendant, or any clothes save what had been huddled on
in haste, nor perhaps even a bed, for we knew that St.
Germain was dismantled of furniture, and that no preparations had been made for fear of giving alarm.

Madame de Fiesque declared that she should die if
she tried to pass the streets of Paris, where we began
to hear loud cries. The maids seemed to have all run
away, and she implored me to go, with all that was most
necessary, to Mademoiselle.

"You are English! You are a very Gildippe. You
have been in the wars—you fear nothing," said the poor
woman. "I implore you to go!"

And as I had my son with me, and it seemed to be

a duty or even a charity that no one else would under-
take, though it was not likely that any harm could come
to us, I sent Gaspard to dress himself, with my faithful
Nicolas, who had come to light. The gentleman undertook to find us Mademoiselle's coach, and we hurried
back to get together what we could for our mistress. I
laugh now to think of Madame de Fiesque and myself
trying with our inexperienced hands to roll up a mattress
and some bedding, and to find the linen and the toilet
requisites, in which we had but small success, for the
femmes de chambre kept everything, and had all either
run away or slept too far off to hear us. We managed at
last to fasten up the mattress with the other things in it,
tied by a long scarf at each end, and dragging it to the
top of the stairs we rolled it down each flight. At the
second it upset an unfortunate lackey, who began to yell,
firmly persuaded that it was a corpse, and that the
Frondeurs had got in and were beginning a general
slaughter.

How we recovered from the confusion I do not know,
but Gaspard joined me at the top of the stairs, bringing
with him a page of his own age, the little Chevalier de
Méricour, whom he entreated me to take with us. All
the other boys had relations close at hand; but this
child's mother was dead, and his father and brothers with
the army. Being really a cousin of Harry Merrycourt's,
he had always seemed like a relation, and he was Gas-

pard's chief friend, so I was very willing to give him a
seat in the carriage, which came from somewhere, and
into which the mattress was squeezed by some means or
other.   Off we set, but no woman of any rank would
accompany me, for they said I had the courage of an
Amazon to attempt to make my way through the mob
that was howling in the streets.

It certainly was somewhat terrible when we came
out into the street thronged with people carrying lanterns
and torches, and tried to make our way step by step.
We had not gone far before a big man, a butcher I should
think, held up a torch to the window, and seeing my
son's long fair hair, shouted, "The King! the King!
Here is the Queen carrying away the King and the Duke
of Anjou!"

The whole mob seemed to surge round us, shrieking,
screaming, and yelling ; some trying to turn the horses,
others insisting that we should alight.   No one heard
my assurances that we were no such personages, that this
was Mademoiselle's carriage, and that the Queen was
gone long ago ; and, what was more fortunate, their ears
did not catch young Méricour's denunciations of them as
vile *canaille*.   A market woman mounted on the step,
and perceiving the mattress, screeched out, " The Cardinal
—they are carrying off the Cardinal rolled up in a
mattress !"

Their fury was redoubled.   I began to untie it to

show them there was nothing, but we had drawn the knots too tight, and Gaspard's little sword would not of course cut, nay, the gleam of it only added to the general fury. I really think if the Cardinal had been there they would have torn him to pieces. They were trying to drag open the doors, and would have done so much sooner but for the crowds who were pushed against them and kept them shut. At last there seemed to be some one among them with a more authoritative tone. The pressure on the door lessened, and it was to my dismay torn open; but at that moment my son called out, "M. Darpent! Oh, M. Darpent, come to my mother!" Immediately M. Clément Darpent, unarmed and in his usual dress, with only a little cane in his hand, made his way forward. Before I saw him I heard his welcome voice calling, "Madame de Bellaise here! I am coming, M. le Marquis! The Queen! *Bêtise!* I tell you it is a lady of my acquaintance."

"The Cardinal! She is carrying off the Italian rolled up in a mattress! Down with the fox!" came another terrible outcry; but by this time M. Darpent had been hustled up to the door, and put himself between us and the throng. He could hear me now when I told him it was merely Mademoiselle's bedding which we were carrying out to her. He shouted out this intelligence, and it made a lull; but one horrid fellow in a fur cap sneered, "We know better than that, Monsieur! Away with traitors! and those who would smuggle them away!"

"Oh! show it to them!" I cried; and then I saw a face that I had known in the hospital, and called him by name. "Jean Marie, my good friend, have you your knife to cut these cords and show there is nothing inside?"

The man's honest face lighted up. "Hein! the good tall lady who brought me *bouillons!* I warrant there is no harm in her, brothers! She's a good Frondeuse, and has nothing to do with foreign traitors."

He ranged himself beside Clément Darpent, offering a big knife, wherewith in a moment the bands were cut and the mattress held up to view, with a few clothes inside.

I made my two defenders understand that they were Mademoiselle's garments, and when this was repeated there was a general shout: "Vive la bonne dame! Vive Mademoiselle! Vive Monsieur! Vive la Fronde!"

Jean Marie, who had worked in a furniture shop, would have rolled up the bed in a trice much better than before, but M. Darpent observed that as we were not yet out of Paris it might bring us into trouble, and, inconvenient as it was, he advised us to keep it open till we were beyond the gates. He asked permission to accompany me to prevent any further annoyance, and Jean Marie, to the extreme disgust of the servants, mounted the box, to serve as an additional guard.

No one could be kinder than M. Darpent. He was very sad about this flight of the Court. He said he feared it was the beginning of a civil war, and that he had thought better of the blood royal and *noblesse* of France than to suppose they would assist a Spanish woman and an Italian priest to trample down and starve their fellow-countrymen in the name of a minor king. He expected that there would be a siege, for he was sure that the temper of the people was averse to yielding, and the bourgeois put their trust in the archers.

I asked if he thought there would be any danger, thinking that I would either join my mother and sister or endeavour to fetch them away; but he assured me that they would be perfectly safe. Was not the Queen of England left, as I assured him, and the Duchess of Longueville ? M. le Prince would allow no harm to touch the place where lived the sister he so passionately loved. I might be secure that the Hôtel de Nid de Merle was perfectly safe, and he would himself watch to see that they were not annoyed or terrified. He gave me the means of writing a billet to my mother from his little Advocate's portfolio, and he promised himself to convey it to her and assure her of our safety, a message which I thought would make him welcome even to her. He was most kind in every way, and when we came near the gate bethought him that the two little boys looked pale and hungry, as well they might. He stopped the carriage near a baker's shop, which was already open, and going in himself, returned with not only bread, but a jug and cup of milk. I think we never enjoyed any- thing so much; and in the meantime the excellent Jean Marie rolled up our mattress so close that, as Gaspard said, it could hardly have been supposed to contain a puppy dog.

They saw us safely through the barriers. M. Darpent gave his word for us, and out we went into the country while scarcely the dawn was yet seen. At a turn in the road we saw only the morning star hanging like a great lamp in the east, and I showed it to the little boys, and told them of the three kings led by the Star to the Cradle. I heard afterwards that the little Chevalier thought we saw the real Star in the East sent to guide us to St. Germain, forgetting that it was the wrong direc- tion; but he had been very little taught, and this was the first he had ever heard of the Gospel, which was familiar to my boy. They both fell asleep presently on the cushions, and I think I did so likewise, for I was surprised to find myself at St. Germain in broad daylight. Everybody was gone to mass for the festival, and we crept in after them.

Mademoiselle was delighted to see me, and always believed we had made our passage so safely in consequence of the respect paid to her and her carriage. It was a strange day; no one did anything but run about and hear or tell news of how the people in Paris were taking the departure of the Court, and wonder when the troops would come up to begin the siege, or, what was more pressing, what was to be done for food and for bedding. We ate as we could. Eggs and fowls were brought in from the farms, but plates and dishes, knives and forks, were very scarce. Some of us were happy when we could roast an egg in the embers for ourselves, and then eat it when it was hard enough, and I thought how useful Annora would have been, who had done all sorts of household work during the troubles at home. But we were very merry over these devices.

The night was a greater difficulty. Most of the windows had no frames nor glass in them, and hardly any one had a bed. Mademoiselle slept in a long gallery, splendidly painted and gilt, but with the wind blowing at every crevice through the shutters, no curtains; only a few marble tables against the wall by way of furniture, and the mattress spread upon the floor for her and her youngest sister, who would not sleep unless she sang, and who woke continually.

I rolled up my two little boys in my great fur cloak, which I had happily brought with me, for no one seemed disposed to take any charge of poor little Méricour, and Nicolas fetched me the cushions from the carriage, so that they were tolerably comfortable.

As to us ladies and gentlemen, we rejoiced that at

least faggots could be had. We made up a great fire,
and sat round it, some playing at cards, others playing at
games, telling stories, or reciting poetry, interspersed with
the sillier pastime of love-making. Every one nodded
off to sleep, but soon to wake again,—and, oh, how stiff
we were, and how our bones ached after two such nights !

And the saddest and most provoking thing, at least
to many of us, was the high spirits of the Queen-Regent.
To be sure, she had not been without a bed in an
unglazed room all night, and had a few maids and a
change of clothes, but she had probably never been so
much out of reach of state in her life, and she evidently
found it most amusing. She did not seem to have an
idea that it was a fearful thing to begin a civil war, but
thought the astonishment and disappointment of the
Parisians an excellent joke. Grave and stately as she
was by nature, she seemed quite transformed, and laughed
like a girl when no gold spoon could be found for her
chocolate and she had to use a silver one. Yes, and she
laughed still more at the ill-arranged limp curls and
tumbled lace of us poor creatures who had sat up all
night, and tried to dress one another, with one pocket-
comb amongst us all !

All that day and all the next, however, parts of
different people's equipages kept coming from Paris.
Mademoiselle's were escorted by Madame de Fiesque,
who had been so civilly treated that Mademoiselle gave

passports for the Queen's waggons to come through Paris ; and it was considered to be a great joke that one of the *bourgeois,* examining a large box of new Spanish gloves, was reported to have been quite overcome by the perfume, and to have sneezed violently when he came to examine them.

We were in a strange state up there on the heights of St. Germain. Some of the Court had no hangings for their great draughty rooms, others had no clothes, and those who had clothes had no bedding. Very few of us had any money to supply our wants, and those who had soon lent it all to the more distressed. The Queen herself was obliged to borrow from the Princess Dowager, even to provide food, and the keeping up of separate tables was impossible. We all dined together, King and Queen, Monsieur, Madame, and all, and the first day there was nothing but a great *pot au feu* and the *bouilli* out of it ; for the cooks had not arrived. Even the spoons and knives were so few that we had to wash them and use them in turn. However, it was all gaiety on those first days, the Queen was so merry that it was every one's cue to be the same ; and as to the King and the Duke of Anjou, they were full of mischief; it was nothing but holiday to them to have no Court receptions.

At eight o'clock in the evening there came a deputation from Paris. They were kept waiting outside in

the snow while the Queen considered whether to receive
them; and she could hardly be persuaded to allow them
to sleep under shelter at St. Germain, though on the road
at that time of night they were in danger from brigands,
travelling soldiers, and I know not what!

They were at last admitted to the ranger's lodgings,
and had an interview with the Chancellor, who was
harsh and peremptory, perhaps feeling himself avenged
for his troubles and fright on the day of the barricades.

When I heard that the President Darpent was among
the deputation I sent Nicolas to find out whether his son
were there; and by and by I received a little billet,
which excited much more attention than I wished.
Some told me I was a Frondeuse, and M. le Baron de
Lamont pretended to be consumed with jealousy. I had
to explain publicly that it was only from my sister, and
then they pretended not to believe me. It was in
English, a tongue of which nobody knew a single word,
except that scandal declared that the Duke of Bucking-
ham had taught the Queen to say "Ee lofe ou;" but it
said only: "We are quite well, and not alarmed, since
we know you are safe. We had heard such strange
rumours that my mother welcomed our friend as an angel
of consolation."

I translated this to all whom it concerned; but M.
de Lamont annoyed me much with his curiosity and incredulity. However, when I found that the unfortunate

deputies were permitted to spend the night in the guard-room I sent Nicolas to see whether he could be of any use to the Darpents. Truly it was a night when, as the English say, one would not turn out one's enemy's dog, and the road to Paris was far from safe; but the ranger's house was a wretched place for elderly men more used to comfort than even the *noblesse*, whose castles are often bare enough, and who are crowded and ill accommodated when in waiting at the palaces.

At that moment a bed was to ourselves a delightful luxury, which Madame de Fiesque and I were to share, so Nicolas could not do much for poor old Darpent, whom he found wet through from having waited so long in the snow, melting as it fell; but he did lend him his own dry cloak, and got some hot drink for him. Clément professed himself eternally grateful for this poor attention when in the morning I sent my son with another note in return to be sent to my mother and sister; and he pro-mised to watch over them as his own life.

This was the last communication I had with my family for two months. The Queen had declared that her absence would be only "a little expedition of a week;" but week after week passed on, and there we still were on the hill. The troops could not entirely surround Paris, but they cut off the chief supplies of provisions, and we were promised that this would bring the city to submission in a day or two; but no such thing. I think we were, on the whole, more hungry than those whom we blockaded.

As each set of officials finished their time of waiting they retired, and nobody came to replace them, so our party became smaller from day to day, which was the less to be regretted as our Lent was Lent indeed. Nobody had any money, and provisions ran very short; everybody grumbled but the Queen and Cardinal, and Mademoiselle, who enjoyed the situation and laughed at everybody.

In the intervals of grumbling every one was making love. M. de Juvizy actually was presumptuous enough to make love to the Queen, or to boast that he did. Mademoiselle, I am sorry to say, was in love, or, more truly, in ambition with the Prince of Condé; M. de S. Maigrin was said to be in love with the Princess, M. de Châtillon with Mademoiselle de Guerchy, and so on.

Even I, who had always declared that it was a woman's own fault if she had a lover, did not escape. I had not my mother to shield me, and nobody had any-thing to do, so it was the universal fashion; and M. de Lamont thought proper to pursue me. I knew he was dissipated and good-for-nothing, and I showed the coldest indifference; but that only gave him the opportunity of talking of my cruelty, and he even persuaded Mademoiselle to assure me that he was in earnest.

"No doubt," said I, "he would like to meddle with

the administration of Nid de Merle.   I have no doubt he
is in earnest about that ! "

But there was no escape, as we lived, from being
beset.   We had all to attend the Queen to the Litanies
at the chapel.   She used to remain in her little oratory
praying long after they were finished, Mademoiselle with
her, and, by her own account, generally asleep.   I am
ashamed to say how much chatter, and how many *petits
soins*, went on among those waiting outside.   I used to
kneel, as I heard people say, like a grim statue over my
chair, with my rosary hanging from my hands, for if I
did but hear a rustle and turn my head, there stood M.
de Lamont with a *bonbonnière*, or a bouquet, or an offer
to shield me from the draught, and I could hear a tittering
behind me.

Yet there was enough to make us grave.   In a fight
with the Frondeurs for Charenton, M. de Châtillon, one
of the handsomest and gayest of our cavaliers, was killed.
He was the grandson of the Admiral de Coligny, and was
said to have been converted to the Church by the miracle
of the ducks returning regularly to the pond where the
saint had bound them to come.   I think he must have
made up his mind beforehand.   But it was a great shock
to have that fine young man thus cut down the day after
he had been laughing and dancing in our gallery.   Yet
all people seemed to think of, when everybody went to
condole with his young widow in her bed, was that she

had set herself off to the best advantage to captivate M. de Nemours!

And then came the great thunderbolt—the tidings of the death of the King of England! I knew it would almost kill Eustace; I thought of my poor godmother, Queen Henrietta, and there I was among people who did not really care in the least! It was to them merely a great piece of news, that enabled them to say, "Yield an inch to the Parliament, and see what it will come to."

That kind, dignified, melancholy countenance as I last saw it was constantly before me. The babble of the people around seemed to me detestable. I answered at haphazard, and begged permission of Mademoiselle to keep my room for a day, as I thought I should be distracted if I could not get out of reach of M. de Lamont.

She gave permission, but she said it was an affectation of mine, for how could I care for a sombre old prince whom I had not seen for ten years?

END OF VOL. I.

Printed by R. & R. CLARK, *Edinburgh.*

www.ingramcontent.com/pod-product-compliance
Lightning Source LLC
Chambersburg PA
CBHW030347270326
41926CB00009B/990